At Home in Vermont

Also by Marguerite H. Wolf

RFD Vermont

Of Cabbages and Kings

*The Sheep's in the Meadow,
  Raccoon's in the Corn*

Seasoned in Vermont

Vermont Is Always with You

At Home in Vermont

Marguerite Hurrey Wolf

Illustrated by Mary MacDonnell

The New England Press
Shelburne, Vermont

The New England Press
P.O. Box 575
Shelburne, Vermont 05482

Library of Congress Catalog Card Number: 90-61999
ISBN: 0-933050-85-2

PRINTED IN THE UNITED STATES OF AMERICA

Introduction

My first book, *Anything Can Happen in Vermont*, written twenty-five years ago, described the funny and fortuitous things that happened to our family after we became year-round Vermonters in 1952. Having emigrated from New York City, we were delighted by the beauty and unique personality of the state and its people. Is it still as beautiful? Is it still different from the megalopolis of the eastern seaboard?

In spite of acid rain and salted roads, the maples still flame in October and their sap still rises in March. The sounds and scents of haying are everywhere in July, and snow still covers the ground from Thanksgiving till Easter. But these seasonal attractions are not unique to Vermont.

What still happens in Vermont is Town Meeting on the first Tuesday in March, where anyone can speak his mind and the same few usually do. Bennington Battle Day, on August 16, and the first day of hunting, in November, are holidays, and there are chicken pie suppers in almost every village in September. The town of Williston is still valiantly opposing the Pyramid Mall proposal. There are still country fairs and quilt shows, pig races and strawberry festivals — and where else would a moose fall in love with a cow? The Champlain monster surfaces periodically if not photogenically, and the flatlander tourist is still outwitted by the descendants of the Green Mountain Boys.

Yes, it still happens in Vermont and every other place where independence, self-sufficiency, and integrity are respected.

For George and Allan,
who walked the last long mile together.

Contents

At Home in Vermont

Strike Up the Band

In late February, when the first chickadee changes his song from "chicka-dee-dee-dee" to "spring soon," the avian orchestra begins to tune up in preparation for the concert of love songs. Of course, throughout the winter we have heard the staccato "picks" and "peeks" of the woodpeckers and the rising "jeeah" of pine siskins and the twittering of redpolls, but they are more tympanic than melodic. If you are lucky enough to have cardinals spend the winter with you, as we did in Kansas and as our friends in Burlington, twenty miles west of us do, then you have heard "cheer, cheer" and "purty, purty, purty" in all seasons like woodwinds. One of the nice things about cardinals is that both males and females sing all year.

But on our back road in Jericho, the first real bird song in the moist fields where cattails grow is the "kankaree" of the redwings. It is as much an announcement of spring as the sight of road crews rolling up the snow fences. The red-wings' songs are the warming-up notes of the clarinets in my spring musical ensemble, and soon the robin's "cheer up" cheerily joins them, with the veerys practicing their scales, always in a downward spiral.

Not to be outnumbered by the reeds, a pair of mourning doves with their plaintive "owoo, owoo" are the cellos, endlessly repeating the same mellow notes. In the evening down by the brook, someone is shaking sleighbells. Hundreds of invisible (to me) peepers are swelling their vesper chorus. Occasionally a bullfrog slaps his bass viol. All right, he's not a bird. Neither are the peepers. But they are part of the orchestra, and they take over the night shift after most of the birds have tucked their heads under their wings. We have a few night performers—the occasional tuba hoot of an owl, or a whip-poor-will endlessly repeating his three notes.

I have never heard a nightingale, which is not surprising because that old-world thrush has not crossed the Atlantic. I have been on Berkeley Square in London but not at the right time. We almost heard one in Falsterbö, on the coast of Sweden. We were having dinner with a Swedish family and had been talking about the similarity of their flowers and ours but the difference in bird life. When I said we had no nightingales in Vermont, but we had their thrush cousins, they suggested that we go outside and listen for one. It was a warm summer night, and we wandered through the quiet village enjoying the cool sea breezes, but no nightingale sang on Falsterbö square.

But their American cousins, the wood and hermit thrushes, fill our summer evenings with clear liquid notes that rival the purity of sound of James Galway's golden flute.

4

No orchestra would be complete without drums and every spring our resident ruffed grouse court the females by raising their ruffs, fanning their tails, and beating their wings, producing a hollow, accelerating drumming noise that sounds unfortunately like an ancient motor throbbing into action. Not only would a silent spring be disastrous ecologically and visually, it would deprive us of the best symphony north of Carnegie Hall.

Spring Greens

Before the advent of frozen vegetables and the huge refrigerated trucks that bring Texas lettuce and oranges from Florida and California to the supermarkets of Vermont, spring greens were eagerly awaited and highly touted as a tonic for the winter-weary system. In my childhood, Italian women wandered through the suburbs of New Jersey digging dandelion greens out of our front lawns. My mother didn't care for dandelion greens or, more likely, the chore of washing them in several waters, but she welcomed the women's help in ridding the lawn of "those weeds."

Now, not only am I a dandelion digger, I also check out all early-growing edibles, beginning with the hard brown knobs of the fiddleheads the first weeks of May, when a few green curls are hunching up out of the root stock to the haylike tangle of the chive clumps where, if I poke down through the matted grass, I am rewarded by a few tender emerald spikes of new growth.

7

The first green shoots of snowdrops and the striped green and white leaves of the crocuses bring me to my knees to free them from their winter accumulation of leaves and twigs. Long before the earliest lettuce, radish, or spinach germinates in the garden, the first spears of the daffodils are stabbing their way up through the leaf mold to lift my spirits. The grass on the south side of the barn greens up with the first warm days. The amethyst shoots of the asparagus aren't green, but they taste green with that same fresh, slightly bitter flavor as the fiddleheads. When nights are still cold, the plants grow much more slowly than they do in the more stable warmth of June, and our first lettuce, asparagus, and spinach are stronger in taste. The bitterness of dandelions is a welcome addition to a salad of supermarket iceberg lettuce. The flavor is that of expensive Belgian endive, and it pleases my thrifty soul that it is there for the taking.

Our grandmothers believed that bitter-tasting things are good for you. Was that a holdover from the Puritan ethic that suffering is beneficial, or was it just that most early medicines were intensely bitter? A tonic was what you needed in the spring to startle you out of the winter doldrums. Fortunately, no one is advocating bitter herbs or sulfur and molasses anymore.

Spring itself is tonic enough, the cool ice-tinged air, a haze of green caught in the branches of the "popples," the smell of the damp earth and the upward mobility of a thousand points of green in the garden.

April

Early April is anticipation and hope. It's a double rainbow in the east after the first thunderstorm. While the murky puddles and mud still suck at your boots, you can look up and see a wedge of geese flying north. My mood rises with the sap in the maple trees. A song sparrow bursts out of the cedar tree, and his clear sweet notes are as cool and pure as the white bells of the snowdrops just pushing up through the leaf mold.

Keats spoke of "chilly-fingered spring," and Gladys Taber of *Ladies' Home Journal* wrote, "Spring still wears pockets full of winter." But though there are patches of snow on the north side of everything and the frost is not out of the garden, Keats also said, "Some shape of beauty lifts the pall from our dark spirits." After the doldrums of winter or personal anxiety, there is always some shape of beauty to be seen if you look closely enough.

The silhouettes of trees that were etchings begin to be washed with watercolors as the pink maple buds open and the weeping willows become luminous. Osiers along the road-sides glow deep crimson, and the incredible softness of pussy willows is an annual miracle.

Grandson Morgan arrives for his Easter egg hunt decked out in his choice of Easter finery, his white jacket—now much too small, but still his pride and joy—a new white button-down shirt, a tie (token of formality worn only once or twice a year), enormous yellow sneakers that lace up and are clutched at the bow by ogre jaws, and padded knee bands with monster faces on them around his pant legs "so that when I kneel down to hunt for Easter eggs, I won't get my best pants wet in the mud." It's hard not to feel cheerful around an exuberant tow-headed eight-year-old to whom the world is one continuing Easter egg hunt.

A flock of robins, a whole flock! I know that a few robins stay all year in Burlington, but robins in Jericho are a sign of spring, and I heard the "kankaree" of a red-winged black-bird. The males arrive a few days ahead of the females to stake out their nesting territories. They make a lot of noise about it, but it's a cheerful racket, a spring chorus long before the peepers tune up. The scarlet epaulets are "a thing of beauty." They remind me of some epaulets our son-in-law Steve wore last summer. Debbie had incubated and hatched chicken eggs with her first-grade class, and at the end of the school year she had to bring the young chicks home. They weren't quite feathered out enough to stay outdoors, but on sunny days Debbie carried their wire-covered crate outside and let them run on the grass. Steve picked up two teenage chicks, placed one on each shoulder of his jacket, struck a mock military pose, and saluted. His barnyard "eagles" and pompous facial expression were so much like Qaddafi's or Castro's that we burst out laughing.

The driveway may still be a slough of mud and the lawn may be matted with tired-looking dead grass, but on the south side of the barn the grass is green. One small dandelion is in bloom, and the little pointed buds on the forsythia are beginning to show slits of yellow.

It's not full spring and there may be more snow flurries and cold nights, but the hope is there, and like the verse on the old sundials, "I only mark the hours that shine."

Parenting, Avian Style

Sometimes I think that birds know more about the care and feeding of young than people do. We had a family of tree swallows in our bluebird house last spring. Our creatures never seem to take up residence in the spaces intended for them. Our two pigs live in what was once part of the milking parlor, and the other end of that area is occupied by twenty laying hens and a male chauvinist rooster whose life has been spared so far only because he is so handsome that I can't bear the thought of dunking those glossy iridescent feathers in hot water. There hasn't been a cow or even a stanchion there in twenty-five years.

But back to the tree swallows in the bluebird nest. I saw two identical swallows gathering nesting materials and stuffing them through the hole of the bluebird house for several days in late May. During the incubation period, we would see the female's head peeking out from time to time, and she occasionally would swoop out for a quick bite of bugs and then back to the nest. Pretty soon both parents were in and out, back and forth, trying to appease the chattering and squeaking babies. Can you imagine how many gnats, black flies, and mosquitos it takes to nourish a baby swallow?

As the young ones grew bigger and feathered out, we'd see a small navy-blue head peeking out, bright shoe-button eyes shining, only to pop out of sight if you came near the nest. Then one day the parents flew frantically in circles around the bird house, over to the fence, and up to the electric wire, all the time calling to the young ones. First one fledgling came out, wobbled, fluttered, and made it to the fence, where he clung swaying back and forth. Mom and Pop cheered and showed him how it's done, and he fluttered after them to another wire. Back they came for the second one, circling, urging, scolding, until he too came halfway out of the round hole, took a fearful look down at the ground, and flapped to the nearest fence post. The next day the box was empty, and there wasn't a tree swallow in sight. We removed the front of the nesting box and lifted out the round straw-and-grass nest—a fairly sloppy affair, but with no trace of eggshells and no mud like the robins use for plaster. We never saw any one of the four birds again.

A month later we were given a closer and more detailed demonstration of how parenting should be done by a mama goldfinch. We never saw her nest, unfortunately, but one day instead of the usual two pairs of adult goldfinches at our niger seed tube, there were eight birds, including four brownish youngsters as big as their parents clinging and wobbling to the wire that stretches from the house to a maple tree and that supports our assorted feeders. The babies actually looked bigger than the mature birds because their feathers were fluffed out, and they flapped their wings constantly trying to keep their balance. They complained loudly too, begging for food. The mother bird would take a mouthful of niger seed, fly up next to one of the young, and stuff it into his gaping, pink-lined beak. Whereupon his siblings would shriek, "Unfair! Me too!" and avian variations on the same theme.

But Mama's role was not just stuffing these big, demanding babies. She was determined to teach them to fly too. When they sidled up next to her on the wire, she flew off to a nearby branch. They squawked piteously, then flopped and wavered after her to the branch. Did she give them a gold star or even a partially digested niger seed? No, she immediately flew back to the wire, and they wobbled and wavered and flew back to her. You could almost feel her insistence that they practice and get their wings in shape for the trip south. For two days she flew from branch to branch, making them follow her and feeding them at intervals. On the third day the boldest one made it to the tube feeder and, with wings still fluttering, helped himself to niger seed. From then on, their flight smoothed out, if you can call a goldfinch's undulating flight smooth. All of them—two males still resplendent in canary yellow and black, two females more somberly dressed, and the four fat brown-with-white-wing-bars young—all fed and argued together at the feeder. Then one day they were gone, swooping off farther south on capable, strong young wings.

We thought that was the last of the goldfinches for the season, but almost two months later the chickadees at our sunflower seed feeder were joined by a solitary male goldfinch. Were some goldfinches staying for the winter?

Fran Howe, our local bird expert, told me that we have goldfinches year round here, but they aren't the same ones. The new gentleman probably came "south" from Canada, and our family is presumably wintering in a sunnier clime.

I hope they all come back next spring. There is no more exhilarating sign of spring than the sight of goldfinches in early March. They are slightly mangy looking while in the midst of changing out of their winter clothes, but the brilliant yellow breeding plumage is well worth the wait.

Vermont
Tree Houses

   Tree houses are not indigenous to Vermont, but with increasing city and suburban construction restrictions, they are now more likely to be found in rural areas.

   Yearning for a tree house tightens the throat and resolve of a ten-year-old boy when the parental roof seems to have too much overhang, yet it is still comforting to be within reach and smell of the kitchen.

   A similar unease, known as horse fever, afflicts girls at about the same age. I'm not sure what the significance of the horse phase is and I'd rather leave it to the Freudians to decide, but I know what the tree-house hunger is all about from firsthand experience. I wasn't a boy when I was ten, but I nearly convinced my parents and the neighborhood boys that I was. Somehow I promoted the idea of a tree house in the big sweet cherry tree that dominated our backyard. I had the dream, the tree, and some scrap lumber in the cellar.

It was a neighbor boy who had the know-how. He already had an asymmetrical hut behind the raspberry bushes at the far end of his yard, which gave him special fifth-grade distinction.

Anticipation comes first, the intoxicating thought of having a hideaway of your own, inaccessible to such predators as unfriendly dogs, piano teachers with metronomes, and elderly relatives whose conversation falters after they have established your age, grade in school, and growth since the last dreary encounter.

Next comes a vortex of feverish activity, lining up parental approval, lumber, tools, and sandwiches and cookies for lunch (and as a hedge against imminent starvation).

It never occurs to the young that the construction of a tree house keeps them busy and out from underfoot for the whole summer. Why else would parents and older sisters cherish tree houses, if not for the respite from slamming screen doors and invasions of hollow-legged grubby friends?

There are certain fundamental requirements for a soul-satisfying tree house. The platform needs to be high enough to be well above the eye-level and reach of the tallest adult, but low enough that the co-owners can scramble up the rope ladder and pull it up behind them before the hot breath of imaginary pursuers is felt upon their necks. It doesn't matter that the treehouse dweller is rarely chased, except by his friends. He enjoys the tingling sense of danger narrowly averted by a burst of speed and the simian agility that leaves his enemies raging helplessly below. A roof of some kind keeps out the elements and protects supplies that have been squirreled away. Besides, a tight tree house is a great place on a rainy day for learning magic tricks, trying

17

the first pine needle cigarette, and holding secret meetings.

This need for privacy is somewhat baffling to parents. What sinister plans require all that scuttling and whispering? Not a plot for annihilation of family or school—simply the urge to share a private world, a badge or emblem, a banding together to reinforce his sense of worth and fiefdom. Is this so different from the rituals that can be observed in fraternal and service clubs of adults in every culture?

Maybe the need for a tree house isn't so childish after all. Maybe he is growing up and wants to loosen the apron strings, firm up a few attachments among his peers, and pull away from the amorphous crowd to a spot where he can conduct a private life less regimented by the so-called civilized world.

Isn't that what brought a lot of us to Vermont or kept us here? No man is an island, but who among us doesn't yearn for one? And if islands are scarce in many neighborhoods, trees are not. The spiritual descendants of the Swiss Family Robinson are still alive and building tree houses in Vermont.

Wildlife—and Death—
in the Country

There is something about the presence of three small grandsons in our semirural environment that lures the wildlife right out of the underbrush. Skunks and woodchucks are always with us. We rarely see the skunks, except squashed on the highways, but we see the little holes they have dug hunting for grubs during the night on our lawn. We keep a respectful distance from skunks, and we fence our garden to keep the woodchucks at a respectful distance from our vegetables. It doesn't always work. A woodchuck can easily dig under a fence if he is highly motivated. This year the weeds were very high both outside and just inside of the fence. Do you suppose they couldn't see the fruits of my labor, or have they moved to greener pastures?

We see only one or two deer each year, and I have gone a whole summer without spying a snake. That suits me just fine. I have trouble appreciating snakes and would welcome a return visit from Saint Patrick. Wouldn't you know that our number-two grandson, Peter, is a dedicated herpetologist? He is surprisingly knowledgeable about snakes and was in seventh heaven in the Everglades one winter vacation.

Whenever Peter is in Vermont, his top priority—after buying up every baseball card in Chittenden County—is to keep an ever-vigilant eye for a snake. He can find them in the grass or on a rock on top of Mount Mansfield. One day, when Patty and her two boys and Debbie with her eight-year-old, Morgan, were walking along the river road, Peter saw a snake in the middle of the road. There is a lot of traffic on that road, and Peter was worried about the snake's chances of survival. He was determined to remove it from the danger zone. Patty was equally worried about Peter's chances of survival and was determined to do the same for Peter. Morgan, who welcomes excitement of any kind, was leaping up and down, shouting, "Get the snake, Peter! Go ahead! Get the snake!" "No!" Patty shouted. "Get out of the road, Peter!" Patrick, at thirteen, the senior grandson and the most controlled, took up a post at a distance down the road and flagged cars down, calling out, "Slow down! There's a snake in the road!" Hardly an emergency in the motorist's mind, but the average motorist doesn't want to run over small boys either.

It was touch and go for a few minutes, with Peter willing to sacrifice himself to save the snake, Patty unwilling to sacrifice Peter for any reason, and Morgan delighted with the general excitement and dramatic turn of events. No lives were lost. I'm glad I only had to hear about it later. The snake and the cars went their separate ways, and pulse rates gradually returned to normal.

One morning shortly after the episode of the snake, Patty and the boys were awakened at six by a loud thump in the road in front of the Cochrans' house. A deer had been hit by Gerry Desso in his brand-new (40 miles only) Buick. Gerry went on to Desso's store to report it to the game warden. A woman in another car stopped and was comforting the badly injured deer, cradling its head and talking to it softly. Her soothing manner with the deer had the same effect on Patty and the boys as they waited for the game warden. The deer was too badly hurt to recover and was quickly shot by the game warden and sold to Gerry for five dollars for a friend. "Sort of sad, but sort of exciting" was Patrick's reaction.

The feistiest bit of wildlife that the boys encountered was also the smallest—a hairy-tailed mole not more than four inches long who was prepared to do battle with all comers. They prudently put on heavy gloves when handling him, but he did his best to bite through the gloves and squeaked at them angrily. Peter, who is omnivorous like the mole, was impressed to read in the *Field Guide to Mammals* that this small creature can consume three times his weight in twenty-four hours. Of course, he goes at it night and day. So would Peter, if he could convince his mother.

They had recently spent part of their vacation in the Olympic National Park and had seen a wide variety of wildlife—a mother bear and cub, elk, deer, Olympic marmots, Townsend chipmunks, and Washington ground squirrels. They enjoyed the tameness of the small rodents and got good pictures of all of them. Of course, they couldn't bring any of those home, but they do have a small furry friend, a quiet little hamster who could fit into a teacup in spite of his name, Thunder. When they came to Vermont last summer, they couldn't find a pet-sitter for Thunder, so he came too, in his natural habitat—a large glass terrarium that seems to house nothing but shredded paper. The paper rises and falls gently as Thunder snoozes away most of the day, becoming sociable only at night. If I can't bring myself to share Peter's enthusiasm for reptiles, I certainly can enjoy cuddling a warm, velvety handful of Thunder.

Summer Rain

You don't have to be Gene Kelly to feel like "singin' in the rain." There are times when a summer thunderstorm rains on your parade or picnic, but most of the time "it droppeth as the gentle rain from heaven upon the place beneath" and, like mercy, is twice or even thrice blest. It raises the water table, refreshes the garden, and settles the dust on the road.

I have happy memories of summer rain. When I was seven years old, I used to go fishing with my father on the Kennebec River, near Hinckley, Maine. Mr. Orvis would not have approved of our gear — a can of worms, which my father kindly put on my hook, a line adorned only with a little lead sinker and hook, and a pole for me that had recently been a birch sapling. We rowed slowly along under the overhanging alders at the shoreline and caught perch and, once in a while in the deeper water, a black bass. Sometimes in a grassy shallow cove tangled with you-know-who's weed, we'd get a pickerel.

But the best part was the expedition itself, digging the worms, assembling a lunch of peanut butter sandwiches, and setting off into the unknown with no destination, just to explore the river like Mole and Water Rat in *The Wind in the Willows*. I remember one day especially because it began to rain when we were at least a mile up the river from our dock. If I had been back at the cottage, my mother would have made me come in. The rain didn't seem to bother my father a bit. In fact, he called it perfect fishing weather. Drops ran off my nose. The cuff of my upturned gob's sailor hat filled with water and overflowed when I leaned over. My shirt clung to my back, and I reveled in the novelty of this almost illicit adventure.

Rain is ignored in the British Isles. Nobody stops playing golf in Scotland. The people of Ireland accept the daily Irish Mist as a guarantee that the Emerald Isle will live up to its name. Swathed in Harris tweed, mackintoshes, and Wellingtons, the English tramp over the hills of Grasmere undaunted by the damp. And in Hawaii you can see rainbows every day, which the residents take for granted and the tourists try to photograph.

Swimming in the rain in our pool at the waterfall adds a whole new dimension of wetness. If it is raining hard, the drops bounce back in the air and the surface is stippled with silver. Getting soaked is redundant when you're already wet.

Once in a while we have a hailstorm in the summer. I've never seen the hailstones as big as the golf balls that the meteorologists talk about. In fact, I don't welcome hail at all—especially in the garden. One summer a freak hailstorm ruined crops of squash, strawberries, and immature tomatoes in the truck gardens in Colchester. In the following days

summer squash with pockmarks was offered for sale at reduced prices in the local supermarkets in an effort to salvage something from the disaster, but the green tomatoes and berries were too badly damaged to save.

From a child's point of view any weather aberration is exciting. One summer when our girls were little, we had a hailstorm. Little icy snowballs the size of BBs plinked on the roof, rattled against the windows, and bounced onto the lawn. The girls were enchanted and rushed out, scooping them up and bringing them in to put in the refrigerator. The stones weren't big enough to really hurt, but being pelted by them took a bit of fortitude. In a few minutes the sun came out, and the hailstones vanished in the grass. Even the dishful in the refrigerator was soon a puddle, but the memory lingered on as the girls compared notes with their friends on the size of their hailstones.

When a serious drought is broken by summer rain, it evokes more than just singing. I have seen tired farmers in South Dakota just standing outdoors with upturned faces shouting their relief. It's more than pennies from heaven, it's dollars. And even here in Jericho in midsummer, when we begin to worry about the well, the plants droop in the garden, the pea vines turn yellow prematurely, and the lettuce bolts, the rumble of thunder and the soft sound of rain in the night start a song in my heart.

Year of the Raccoon

I don't care what the Chinese calendar calls it, 1989 was the Year of the Raccoon in Jericho Center. Of course the raccoons are always with us, but this year the raccoons and the Wolfs had more close encounters than either enjoyed.

How many raccoons does it take to outwit two Wolfs? Only one, with one paw tied behind his fur coat. Actually I like the masked bandits 11 months of the year. In the winter, if we turn on the porch light at night, we often see one standing on his hind legs prying sunflower seeds out of the bird feeder. We can stand only a few inches away from him as long as we stay on the inside of the window. But the minute we open the door, he waddles off into the woods with his funny bearlike gait. Raccoons' faces are attractive. They look intelligent, and they are. They look friendly, but they are not. They don't look devious, but they are.

During the month of August, my admiration for raccoons

goes into reverse. A week or so before the corn is ready to eat, one furry scout will rip off a few ears, examine them, and discard them as too immature. There may be a respite of a week or so, but then they decide it is ready. Now, don't suggest putting pumpkins in the corn. Our corn patch is as vigorously entwined as Laocoön and his sons. You can't walk barelegged through the corn without being prickled pink. Electric fence? We've tried it—it worked two years out of eight. Human hair? No luck. I salvaged a bag of it from my friend and hairdresser, Pam Tatro, but the human scent must have been washed out with the shampoo, because it didn't give the raccoons a moment's pause. A radio in the garden? Come on! The average raccoon would be so curious, he'd be switching stations all night. Crank case oil? Do you really want it on your shoes? A dog? Yes, probably—but I don't want to care for and feed a dog all year in exchange for his raccoon-deterrent talents in August.

Of course, if George were willing to sit up all night in the garden with a rifle across his knees, he might pick off one or two, but he seems strangely uninterested in that idea.

We've kept chickens for years. They have relatively free, albeit indoor, range in the barn. That's to discourage a variety of predators—skunks, weasels, and foxes, as well as raccoons. We caught a weasel once, an ermine really, because of his winter pelage, and George and a skunk surprised each other in the chicken coop one morning. They each backed off slowly without incident. This year, besides our "old girls" (laying hens), we adopted fifteen young chickens that Debbie had hatched at school for the enlightenment of her first-graders. We had hoped to add them to our flock, but old girls never take kindly to new kids on the block. The year before, both the old and the new were identical in color—red—and after the usual period of hazing, keeping the new girls away from feed and water and shoving them off the roost, the new ones were finally accepted. This year the young ones are white, and when they were small, we knew they would be pecked to death by our resident fowl. So we put them in a raised cage that had quarter-inch wire mesh on all sides, top, and bottom. All went well for a while, but then one morning we found a dead pullet. A raccoon (we assumed) had reached up through a narrow space where the fencing met, pulled down a leg, and eaten the leg, the thigh, and part of the breast. We set the Hav-a-Hart trap in the chicken barn, and lo and behold! next morning the appealing masked face was peering out of the trap. George had no heart. The raccoon was shot and buried in the small salad garden adjacent to the barn.

Aha! we thought. We've solved the problem. But there is never only one problem with raccoons. Two nights later, another chicken was mauled through the wire. We set the trap again and caught raccoon number two. That apparently took care of the raccoons who had discovered there were chickens in the barn. Why didn't they go after the old girls, who were much more accessible? The white ones by then were almost as big as the red hens. Maybe the wire cage presented more of a challenge.

That was in July, before the corn season, and in our ignorance we thought perhaps we wouldn't have raccoon predations that year because we'd already caught two. Wrong again. They allowed us to pick and eat several dozen ears, and we basked in false security. Then one morning we found two or three eaten ears. We baited the trap and set it in the garden. Sure enough, two shoe-button eyes peered out of the trap in the morning. We didn't even consider taking him up the road and releasing him on the side of Bolton Mountain. There are quite a few houses on even the most remote road, and if we were seen releasing a raccoon, the local residents would probably form a posse and come after the bad Wolfs. So once again, George shot and buried the raccoon—this time in the main garden, where the corn is, so that he would eventually be recycled and serve at least one useful purpose.

A gardener should never rest on his laurels or his hoe. To keep us from complacency, the next morning I discovered that all the broccoli leaves and a row of lettuce had been eaten. Raccoons don't care for broccoli or lettuce. The garden is fenced, so it wasn't a rabbit. A deer, perhaps—but not too likely here since the hunters have kept our deer population down. It had to be a woodchuck. We patrolled the fence looking for a hole such as we'd found in former years. Nothing. Then, right in the center of the garden, 20 feet from the fence in each direction, under a spreading zucchini plant, we saw a large woodchuck hole and mound of earth. This meant that the chuck had dug a 20-foot tunnel, when he could have gotten into the garden with a simple hole near the fence. Woodchucks aren't as bright as raccoons, and Wolfs aren't as bright as either one. George set off a smoke bomb in the hole, which made enough flame and black smoke to scare us if not the woodchuck. But tender green stuff continued to disappear. So we set the Hav-a-Hart again, and this time the blunt brown face of a woodchuck was pressed against the bars.

Are you keeping track of the number of bullets that George

has used? A raccoon's skull must be made out of granite. George is a good shot, but he hates to see an animal suffer, so he shoots several times in quick succession.

Now, let's see—two raccoons in the barn, one in the garden, and a woodchuck. Maybe that would do it, but just in case, we baited the trap with both fruit for the chucks and fish for the raccoons. You can't say we don't set a gourmet trap.

In the next week we caught two more raccoons, and I picked all the nearly ripe corn. But the raccoons had spread the word that the trap was to be avoided. The next morning the patch of late, unripe corn was strewn with gnawed cobs. I counted 30 discards before I lost interest in the dismal tally. Not a single ear was left.

Why do we bother to raise corn? A sensible question, but don't expect a sensible answer from anyone with earth under his fingernails. As Virgil wrote, "God did not will that the way of cultivation should be easy." He probably was also smart enough to know that every gardener is a compulsive gambler, titillated by the odds.

The Chime of Distant
Wedding Bells

When my parents celebrated their fiftieth wedding anniversary, I thought they were very old. I couldn't picture myself in that situation because at that time my own marriage, of eighteen years' duration, seemed to have lasted half my lifetime. They were in Florida and we were in Vermont, so we didn't attend the reception their friends gave them. But my sister and I, out of a combination of love and guilt, arranged a shower of cards from their distant friends.

Fifty-year wedding anniversary parties have never appealed to either of us. We laugh at the photographs of those couples in the Sunday paper—she often a buxom, elderly Amazon looking as though she'd dragged her reluctant spouse to the photographer's, his expression a mixture of acute embarrassment and surprise at his survival.

But having been married in 1939, we realized, 1989 would make it fifty years whether we liked it or not. We liked the marriage fine, but when Debbie began muttering about an *event,* we pleaded with both girls to let the day pass unobserved.

It happened that Patty, Tage, and their boys were in Vermont for a visit somewhat before the telltale date. Patty told me that Debbie wanted us all to come to her house for dinner one night. I smelled a rat, but I was grateful that it sounded like just a family dinner. The reason for the faint sniff of rodent was that on the phone Debbie said, "Come early so we'll have time for the show. Oh, Lord! Gulp!" When I said, "What?" she quickly countered with, "Oh, nothing. Come early so we can *show* you some pictures." She won't know until she reads this that I heard her the first time.

And what a wonderful show it was! A "This Is Your Life," with Patty and Debbie and the three grandsons acting out various high points in our lives. How they got eight-year-old macho man Morgan into a diaper and carrying a baby bottle as infant George I can't imagine. One of the boys wore cap and gown as George receiving an honorary degree at UVM, and the tableau of me signing books in a bookstore was painfully true and funny.

Patrick, as narrator, read what purported to be a press release to the local paper:

"For the *Burlington Free Press* August 2, 1989. Dr. and Mrs. Wolf celebrated their 50th wedding anniversary at the lovely home of their daughter, Mrs. Stephen Page, in Williston. They renewed their wedding vows under the porch. Many, many relatives attended the party, including their three grandsons, Dudley Chuck Edwardson, Horace Bartholomew Edwinson, and Morris Fenton Edgarson. In the middle of the party the couple left for home.

"When asked their secret for a happy marriage, Dr. Wolf answered, 'None of your goddamn business!'"

34

English Spoken Here

When I was eight years old, we spent the winter in Switzerland. My elderly midwestern grandparents were with us, and after having felt tongue-tied in French and German, they were looking forward to a week in England before we returned to the States. They had both been born in the British Isles but had left in early childhood. Nevertheless, it was the mother country and the mother tongue, and they anticipated the independence that had been denied them in Geneva and Grindelwald. When we landed in South-ampton, a stevedore rushed up to my grandmother and asked her something in a waterfall of cockney phrases, only one word of which she understood. He called her "luv." At least she could read the street signs and the London *Times*, but her communication on the street was minimal.

When I was sixteen, we spent a month in Oxford. Oxonian was easy to understand and fell mellifluously on the ear, but sometimes the meaning eluded me. The greengrocer's boy arrived on his bicycle each morning asking for our order and extolling the freshness of beetroots and marrows. The little maid who came with the house asked my mother to buy her a "reel" of cotton and warned us to "mind the dustbin on the gallery." Lo, it was an ash can on the porch, and we were to avoid it, not to care for it. "Biscuits" were plain crackers or cookies, and "gooseberry fool" was a tart-sweet dessert. A neighbor boy asked my sister and me if we would care to go for "ices," and we agreed, wondering whether it was a skating rink or an Egyptian goddess. It was ice cream with a wafflelike cookie stuck in the top. When he suggested "punting up the river for a game of rounders," I was happily surprised to recognize my childhood game of One-a-Cat. His aunt was an obstetrician, but she saw her patients in her "surgery." He planned to "read history" in university, which meant that history would be his college major. When we asked the man at the railroad ticket office if we could get off at one station and then get back on, he looked totally blank, then said, "Oh, you want to break your journey?"

I thought I had mastered the essential phrases, but thirty years later, when George and I rented a car, you'd think the chief hurdle would be adjusting to driving on the left. Think again. The position of the wheel took care of helping him stay on "the wrong side of the road," but we soon realized anew that English, not American, is the sign language of the road. "Roundabouts" and "lay-bys" we could figure out. At least "tyre" and "tire" sound alike, and so do "kerb" and "curb," but when we were warned that there were "loose chippings ahead," I looked for a lumberyard. We were urged to "filter into a straight line" and were notified of an impending "dual carriageway." We knew that "petrol" was what was in the tank and that the "windscreen" and the "bonnet" were between us and the headlights, but where was the "boot"? And when the next sign advertised "diversion ahead," I expected some sort of entertainment.

Maybe the rental-car agencies at Heathrow and Gatwick should put up signs that read, "American spoken here."

What's So Funny?

Some funny things have happened to us on the way to our present state of happy semiretirement. The usual basis for a comic situation is incongruity. A small child laughs when a grownup falls down because adults normally remain upright. A dog riding a bicycle is considered funny, though not by me—I think it's an insult to the dog, but I'm in the minority on that one. A clown is funny because he wears outrageous clothes and makeup. So was Calvin Coolidge in a feathered Indian headdress. Charlie Chaplin's walk and baggy pants epitomized the shy little guy hoping to look like a big shot.

And some of the funny moments in our life were incongruous situations. The ladies of the chorus in Wagner's *Ring* cycle at the Metropolitan Opera, when viewed from standing room in the peanut gallery when we were students, were eye-opening. They were Rhine maidens or Valkyries in full

38

costume from the waist up, but they were wearing voluminous ski pants, wool socks, and sneakers from the waist down. Most of the audience seated in the orchestra or balcony saw them as authentic warriors, but we saw them as half Valkyries and half well-endowed hausfraus trying to keep warm.

When we lived in Kansas, many of the funny situations were related to the enormous Tudor mansion we lived in. It had a sunken forty-foot living room and a paneled thirty-six-foot dining room presided over by a Waterford crystal chandelier. The chandelier was a very valuable antique. It had been insured twenty years earlier for $4,000. I treated it with respect. So did the housekeeping staff that the medical center sent up to clean the establishment. In fact, they flatly refused to touch it. But it hadn't been cleaned for years, and I pictured it restored to its former sparkling glory. Taking it down was out of the question. You remember about Mohammed and the mountain? It couldn't come down, so I had to go up. My idea had been to remove all the prisms, wash them, and rehang them. But they didn't lift off—they were wired on.

So I took off my shoes, climbed in my stocking feet onto the long refectory table beneath the chandelier, and was almost eye to eye, in fact nicked in the forehead by, the dangling prisms. I carefully washed off every one of those crystals with the solution of vinegar and water that had been prescribed by the attending housekeepers, who hovered around awaiting the demise of either the chandelier or me. It wasn't a lot of fun. It reminded me of attempts at painting a ceiling and the resulting stiff neck. I was glad when the phone rang, but one of the housekeepers answered it.

All I heard was, "I don't think Mrs. Wolf can come to the phone. She's hanging from the Waterford crystal chandelier."

Lots of funny things happened in that house, but most of them have already been told in the chapter called "On Looking a Gift House in the Mouth" in my book *Vermont Is Always With You*. It was, and is, a wonderful and unique house with bees in the walls, a ghost in the dining room, an enormous laundry chute, and an incinerator that had mercifully burned its last before we took up residence. We learned that it had been the cause of several fires.

One item of furniture that arrived there with us was a small plastic electric organ, bigger than a toy but definitely not a product of Messrs. Baldwin or Steinway. We had sold our piano when we left Vermont, so George occasionally picked out a tune or a Christmas carol on the small organ, and it was treated as and sounded like a toy.

One evening, we were invited to dinner by Mr. and Mrs. Milton McGreevy, a distinguished couple influential in Kansas City's philanthropic and cultural circles. Mr. McGreevy was to pick us up. George, ready ahead of time as usual, was hunkered down at the little organ looking exactly like Schroeder in *Peanuts*, playing Beethoven on his toy piano and singing at the top of his lungs. He didn't hear the door chimes. He didn't hear me or Mr. McGreevy come into the room. He was entranced by the sound of his own voice reverberating off the walls.

Mr. McGreevy, a very large gentleman, stood on the threshold and with a perfectly straight face commented, "I had no idea Dr. Wolf was musical!"

One night when George had a meeting in New Haven, he flew into LaGuardia and took the commuter bus that stops at several coastal cities on the way to New Haven.

The driver turned off the highway into Stamford, stopped at the bus depot in town, called out "Stamford!" and waited, expecting someone to get off. No one stirred. After a few minutes the driver announced, "Wake up, folks. This is Stamford!" No response. The driver stood up, looking annoyed, and shouted, "If none of you wanted to get off at Stamford, why didn't you tell me where you didn't want to go before we started?" He was the only one not laughing when they went on.

Another nice moment, which I didn't see but wish that I had, was after we came back to Vermont and once again had chickens in the barn. One morning I found a dead headless hen. The next morning there was another dead hen, the body intact but a small red hole in her neck. Local opinion pointed its finger at a weasel. After the demise of a third bird, we baited the Hav-a-Hart trap with a piece of raw meat. To the astonishment of both the weasel and the Wolfs, the next morning the shoe-button eyes of a beautiful white ermine were glaring out at us with loathing. I wasn't crazy about him either, till I saw how handsome he was in his royal robes.

After George shot him, it seemed a shame just to bury him, even if it had been possible to dig a small grave in the frozen earth. I wanted other people to see him so I froze him in a plastic bag and displayed him to every interested wildlife enthusiast who crossed our threshold. A friend suggested that Lee Allen of the Audubon Society was interested and the ermine might have a second career as a stuffed exhibit for school programs or at the Audubon Center.

So I took our frozen ermine to Dr. Sinclair Allen's office

for him to take home to Lee. Sinclair wasn't there, but his secretary, after recovering from the shock of being handed a dead weasel, offered to put him in a brown bag in the refrigerator, where several of the staff parked their brown bag lunches. You guessed it. Hunger took over before Sinclair returned, and someone opened the brown bag that housed our ermine. Now *that's* a funny moment I wish I had seen!

In Praise of Small Things —Amen!

I would make a terrible Texan. Big is beautiful there, but I'm not convinced. Astrodomes, colossal malls, and ranches that reach out of sight just give me a feeling of agoraphobia. I don't like a sky that is forever. I like it indented by rolling hills and an occasional mountain. Maybe that's because I live in a small house on a small farm in a small state where boiling down—as in maple syrup—improves the flavor.

Throughout the year I am drawn to little things, from the first tiny snowdrop bravely hunching its little bell, through the granular snow, to the last small red leaf clinging to the euonymus bush.

When I was a child, I admired those sets of nested Russian lacquered dolls. I still do. It wasn't the largest, outside one that I coveted. It was the final tiny one, no bigger than a grain of rice. Even in foods, wild strawberries and blueberries have more flavor than the cultivated ones, and caviar is tastier than a goose egg. Little capers, whether the imported ones or the nasturtium seed pods that we pickle for a homemade variety, add a unique piquancy to many dishes. I admire hummingbirds more than ostriches and hope that someday I'll see a hummingbird's nest, that tiny thimble-size invention of lichens, with maybe two tiny pea-size eggs in its little cup.

It is the minuscule mustard seed that is used as a parable in the Bible and also as a symbol of good luck along with a four-leafed clover, rather than a ti leaf.

A bird in the hand is worth a lot more than two in Peterson's field guide. I defy anyone to hold a small bird and not feel moved by the energy in the tiny, amazingly rapid heartbeat. The most blasé tough guy smiles when a baby's starfish hand curls around his finger. The gentle response has more clout than a weightlifter's biceps.

Nothing is more endearing than several kittens hiding and pouncing and leaping up in the air, their little pointed tails upright and velvet paws pummeling each other. I like cats, but even people who profess to dislike cats are melted by the playfulness of kittens.

It often seems that small kindnesses mean the most, the single flower, the person who slows his car to allow you to get out of a driveway, the friend who sends you a clipping about your grandchild.

When Mother Teresa spoke to a grand conference of quantum physicists at the Oberoi Towers Hotel in Bombay, she said, "We can do no great things; only small things with great love."

Pig People

Winston Churchill was a statesman, an artist, and an admirer of pigs. When a friend asked him why he was fond of pigs, Churchill replied, "Dogs look up to you, cats look down on you, but pigs treat you as equals."

Over a period of forty years we have had only two dogs, an embarrassingly large number of cats, and fifty-eight pigs (two at a time, but none during the nine years we lived in Weston, Massachusetts, and Mission Hills, Kansas). If you are familiar with Weston or Mission Hills, you'll know why. We failed as dog people because we didn't include them emotionally as part of the family. Cats, of course, don't mind being taken or left alone. In fact, they prefer to bestow their favors at their discretion.

Because we live in the country, the cats with a few exceptions were primarily barn cats. Mitty was the first one to become a house cat and respected member of the family.

She was a handsome black cat with snow-white paws that gave her her name, and she found us useful and amusing. She honored us by having her kittens in a doll carriage in Patty's room and tolerated our fatuous attention to them with benign condescension. Mr. Cat was a dignified gentleman, coal black and very decorative on our scarlet couch. He came in and out at will—his will, not ours—and added a touch of elegance to a household unremarkable for that quality.

When our girls were little, kittens were their first pets, except for a few goldfish in a New York apartment. The kittens endured all the indignities that two little girls imposed upon them. They were stuffed into doll's clothes and trundled around in a doll carriage, but wasted no time in squirming out of both. Debbie used to wear her kitten. She tucked the lower half of the kitten's anatomy into the elastic waistband of her shorts, allowing the forelegs and head to react to the passing scene as she went about her small business. Oddly enough, the kitten seemed to accept this as normal transportation.

One day a ladder was leaned up against the porch roof. When I noticed that three-year-old Debbie had not been under my feet for some time, I went outside. To my horror Debbie and her kitten were playing on the roof. As calmly as possible I asked her to come down. "Okay," she said, and promptly threw the cat off the roof. After a few aerial somersaults the cat landed on four paws and retired speediy to the barn. Debbie backed down the conventional way and explained, "Patty said cats always land on their feet. I wanted to see her do it."

On another day I looked out of the window just as Mr.

Day, our mail carrier, reached out of his car to open our mailbox. I saw him recoil as though he had received an electric shock. It was a shock all right, but not electric. Debbie had put her kitten in the mailbox and closed it. Confinement did not appeal to the kitten, and she leaped out into Mr. Day's unsuspecting face. Debbie was delighted. The cat and Mr. Day needed a little time to appreciate the humor.

In feeble defense of Debbie's animal husbandry I have to say that as an adult Debbie has been a patient and kind trainer of her golden retrievers. Pathrushin was a loyal friend and constant companion for his eleven years, and now Muff, who is technically Morgan's dog, is an integral part of their family. I didn't tell their cat, Rusty, about Debbie's treatment of cats in her childhood. Rusty had enough to worry about escaping Muff's exuberant advances.

Churchill was right. Dogs do look up to you. Cats do look down on our human frailties, and pigs seem to believe that we are really misshapen pigs who walk on hind legs and were placed on earth to supply them with food. They will supply the entertainment. Pigs are very intelligent. We have never tried to train ours, but there was a sow in Underhill who was housebroken. We do not expect our pigs to emulate Arnold on *Green Acres*, but then, I can't emulate Eva Gabor either. I doubt if a pig wants to act like a human any more than I want to act like a pig. We respect our differences and enjoy each other's company. We nourish them for seven months, then they nourish us for the next seven. It is an equitable arrangement.

Women of Letters

My grandmother was a letter writer, like many of her generation. She wrote every week to each of her six adult children, who were scattered from California to New Jersey. Letters were links that made up the circle of the family in a time before long-distance calls were everyday occurrences. I don't think I ever spoke to my grandmother on the phone, even though I was twenty-two years old when she died.

In contrast, I heard my oldest grandson in Finland cry over the phone when he was a few weeks old. Both he and his brother phone quite casually now that they are living in Connecticut, to ask a question or suggest what they might like for Christmas. And my youngest grandson, who lives only eight miles away, began to use the phone as soon as his fat little fingers could hit the right numbers. Early phone communication with Morgan was minimal because he pressed his mouth against the phone and shouted, so that even by holding the phone a foot away from my ear, I could hardly figure out the slushy message. Now, at eight, he uses a formal approach. "George? This is Morgan. May I please speak to Maggie?" For reasons known only to him, on the phone I'm Maggie. In person, I'm Gramma.

But the point, in case you're wondering if there is one, is that people used to write letters that conveyed description, emotion, and humor, not simply information.

I had a wonderful English teacher in college, Leonora Branch, who wrote entertaining little notes. I wish I had saved them. Debbie wrote very funny letters home from college, and when she was working in New York or traveling in Alaska, Costa Rica, or Ireland. Patty's letters from international work camps in Yugoslavia, Norway, and Finland and her years in Finland and Denmark deserved a wider readership. How I wish I had saved them all! In moving from Vermont to Massachusetts to Kansas and back to Vermont, the letters were victims of the attacks of "the throws" I get when packing.

I have saved letters from two distinguished Vermont writers because they were instrumental in shaping my life. When I was first yearning to have my writing published and I was sending out manuscripts that turned into homing pigeons, I wrote several short historical pieces for the Vermont Historical Society's *News and Notes*. I wasn't paid for them. I didn't expect to be. It was reward enough just to see my words in print. But no one except my mother paid much attention to these efforts.

Then one day in 1958, I received a letter that was a true inspiration. The letterhead was "Dorothy Canfield Fisher, Arlington, Vermont." The date, April 12. "Dear Mrs. Wolf:

I have just had the great pleasure of having one of my readers-aloud (for my old eyes are now so dim I am no longer able to read myself) read your article on Susannah Fay and I am moved to dictate to my secretary a note of appreciation. I am struck by the distinction of your presentation of this early Vermont woman, as much by the excellent, judicious choice of material as by the wholly suitable verbal form you give your portrait. It is fine to know that so able a person as you is willing to write for this little Vermont magazine and I think you may be interested to know that I am sending it down to the English department in our local high school as a perfect example of what this kind of historical writing for our Vermont readers should be. They couldn't have a better one. With best greetings, Dorothy Canfield Fisher."

She continued to write to me from that April to the day before she died, the following November. I have ten little letters. On April 19: "Do go on writing. You have more of a gift than you seem to realize." And on April 17: "If you can possibly arrange your daily life to allow time for writing, I think you ought to do it, because it is seldom I have seen such a rare network of words."

The kindness of a very busy, famous writer past eighty, taking the time to encourage a young unknown writer was overwhelming. I never met Mrs. Fisher, but my girls used to say that if the house burned down, I would have salvaged her letters before my children.

My other beloved Vermont writer friend was Louise Andrews Kent, "Mrs. Appleyard" to most of us. Now, there was a lady who turned letter writing into entertainment! Her letters sounded just like her books, and if you haven't read *Mrs. Appleyard and I*, written when she was eighty, go to the library today.

51

In her first letter to me she wrote, "I love *Anything Can Happen in Vermont*. I bought it with the generous notion of giving it away but I simply couldn't. I'm so grateful to you for writing it. Any time conversation seems to be getting a little morose, I tell your story about the kittens that didn't turn out to be biscuits. The result is all the pleasure I might have given by serving strawberry short cake and none of the trouble."

In another letter she was commenting on my description of our early safaris from New Jersey to Maine in a 1922 Studebaker. "I was able to share the journey with you every inch of the way. By changing the blown out tires quickly and efficiently Rich would get us from Brookline to Kent's Corner in two days. His last gesture, before we left Brookline and he had packed us into the car with bundles to wedge us in safely was to throw in his hat and put on his peaked cap. Sam loved the hat and several times threw it out of the car just for exercise. It made it so embarrassing to keep stopping our covered wagon and reclaiming the hat from mud or dust that when he threw out his own pet pillow, without which he could not sleep, and it sailed pinkly over a bridge rail into a gushing torrent, I never even mentioned it. We drove on briskly until another tire blew out and I discovered that after all Sam *could* sleep without that pink pillow."

I wrote to tell her that we would be unable to come to Kent's Corner on the date she had suggested, and she replied, "'Oh well!' as my youngest grandson said, instead of crying, when he dropped a confection he had just carefully made of peanut butter and marshmallow fluff face down on the floor. I shall have to adopt his philosophy."

And after describing a birthday party, she wrote, "My

husband was splendid at aiming champagne corks, and it was only lately that my son told me that he didn't really need to shoot it into that Chinese bowl on top of the highboy. He just did it to see my expression of ecstasy and dread."

These two women ignited me with Pater's "hard blue flame." I felt an obligation to try to fulfill their expectations. In spite of the telephone company's exhortation to "reach out and touch someone," there is not the same permanence in the spoken word. As Emily Dickinson wrote,

A word that breathes distinctly
Has not the power to die.

Nature's Last Green
Is Gold

Early October in Vermont is so spectacular that when the crimson leaves of the swamp maples and the scarlet and saffron leaves of the sugar maples are spread like oriental rugs beneath the branches, we're apt to think the show is over.

The wave of leaf-peepers recedes, carrying its burden of pictures, maple syrup, cheese, and apples, and once again Vermonters turn their thoughts to winter as the first snow dusts the mountaintops. Pumpkins stand guard on every doorstep, and stuffed scarecrows lounge beside them waiting for Hallowe'en.

It is only after the maples have shed their conflagration that the "popples" and birches take center stage. On every hillside splashes of lemon-yellow poplar and birch shimmer among the dark evergreens. Here and there hickory, butternut, and horsechestnuts spread out amber fingers, and the

burnished steeples of tamaracks reach up to the blue October sky.

"Nature's first green is gold. Her hardest hue to hold," according to Robert Frost. Her last green is also gold, the tawny fronds of ferns recumbent now throughout the woods, pale ecru-colored cornstalks rustling like taffeta in the fields, piles of fat, glossy pumpkins heaped at every roadside stand, goldenrod, dry and brittle, its summer glory faded to mustard. And here and there a last dandelion shining in the grass to assure us that they'll be back a thousandfold in the spring.

Now for six months we'll have to hunt for gold in the afternoon light that washes the western side of every farmhouse and church steeple with pale gold, and in the citrus colors of winter sunsets, lemon yellow, pale orange, and lime at the horizon. Ephemeral gold, to be treasured only for a moment, but a promise that the willow wands will glow again in April and the pastures will be spangled with dandelions in May.

"Nothing gold can stay."

Storing Up

The chipmunk hanging upside down by his hind feet on our tube bird feeder is stuffing his cheek pouches so full that he looks like Dizzy Gillespie playing the trumpet. He feels the urgency of autumn, and so do I, the compulsion to store up every available seed for the winter.

From that first cool day at the end of August when we dug the potatoes, spreading them out on the ground to cure for a day, I have been intermittently nudged by this need to gather and hoard everything in the garden. Digging potatoes is like an Easter egg hunt. It is a delightful surprise to pull and dig up a withering plant and find five or six big fat potatoes and a handful of baby ones to eat right away, along with the ones you stab by mistake.

Of course, harvesting starts much earlier than that, way back in June when the asparagus shot up faster than two people could eat it even at the rate of two meals every day.

Have you a recipe for asparagus for breakfast? In an omelette maybe, although George has conservative tastes in food and has never expressed a hankering for green things before noon. We don't like frozen asparagus much, but chopped before blanching, it makes a lovely green soup base to freeze for a February lunch.

There never are enough peas to freeze. There never are enough peas, period. I can't understand it. This year I planted three varieties—early, late, and sugar-snap—but we just ate them happily as soon as they filled out and sometimes before. I like everything about peas, their pewter-textured blue-green color, their prehensile tendrils reaching out for anything to embrace, and their wonderful fresh flavor. I don't even mind shelling them. I like the plink of the peas in a pan and the rich green smell of the satiny pods. The pods look good enough to eat, and in the case of sugar-snap or snow peas they are, but I've always been puzzled by the fact that neither our sheep nor our chickens nor our pigs will eat them. Wouldn't you rather eat a succulent pea pod than dry grain?

Fall is the time when I am possessed by the storing demon. The onions have been pulled, dried, and hung in mesh bags. We use up the thick-stemmed ones right away. They don't keep well. We haven't bought an onion for many years except for an occasional red or Vidalia one. That gives me a sense of self-sufficiency, illusory but satisfying.

Toward the end of September, we load the garden cart with buttercup squash and pumpkins and line them up in the garage. We have solved the problem of peripatetic winter squash wandering all over the garden and looking unpleasantly like that famous sculpture of Laocoön and his sons entangled by serpents. We plant them outside the garden in a patch of their own. There they can wrap around the neighboring weeds at will and climb up a flowering crab tree without annoying me. In fact, I like to see those plump dark-green flying saucers swinging from the branches. They startle our city-bred friends, and that amuses us simple country types. None of our hungry furry friends—rabbits, woodchucks or even voles—show any interest in winter squash.

After I've made dill pickles and bread-and-butters with the cucumbers, I make our favorite end-of-the-garden relish with cabbage, green tomatoes, onions, and peppers. It satisfies my thrifty streak to use up quite a lot of those green tomatoes, and I love the smell of the salted vegetables sitting on the kitchen counter. I don't even like to turn on the kitchen fan when I'm making pickles. I like to step into a house that is redolent of onions, cucumbers, vinegar, and spices.

Children are natural fall hoarders. I'd be suspicious of a child who didn't dart after one more especially crimson maple leaf and come home with a fistful of scarlet, gold, persimmon, and apricot treasures. As a child I couldn't resist gathering horsechestnuts. I really had no use for them. I just enjoyed the satiny smooth texture and glowing color.

My grandfather used to send us a barrel of apples from his farm in Michigan each fall—Northern Spies, Jonathans, and Grimes Goldens. I used to hang over the rim of the barrel in the cellar and sniff their fruity breath. My mother always canned peaches and cherries. I don't can any fruits, I freeze them, but I remember her throwing a dish towel over the hot jars just in case one of them exploded. They never did, but it was a long process in the days before pressure canners to boil the jars, both before and after they were filled. She was proud of the jars on the cellar shelves. I feel the same way about our pickles and jellies. Somehow, a full freezer doesn't give me the same visual satisfaction. Perhaps it's because you can't see the product. Stacks of white packages don't give the same aesthetic pleasure as light glowing through a jar of currant jelly.

I know how our chipmunk feels. He won't eat half of the seeds he is storing away. He may not remember where some of them are, but right now he and I are responding to an atavistic need to gather and store before the long winter sleep.

Things I Can Live Without

I had always thought that the Neiman-Marcus Christmas catalogue contained the least needed and most expensive gifts for those on your list who have everything except restraint. But now Hammacher-Schlemmer is running a close second. I have to admit that their items are useful. They *do* something. In fact, my complaint is that they do more than I want to have done to me. Their slogan—"New York's most famous store since before the Civil War"—makes me wonder what Messrs. H and S would have thought of some of these current offerings.

Now, don't misunderstand me. We have a good many of their excellent products in our house, and we use them all the time—a hand vacuum which we call a "fly sucker," a step-on can, and a folding coat rack. The plate warmer gets only occasional use. But I have this mental image of their think tank on East Fifty-seventh Street dreaming up items no one has ever tried to sell before and that everyone can live without.

I will start with the least expensive—at $19.95, probably the lowest price in the catalogue. For that pittance you may become the proud owner of a triple-action space pen that writes upside down, in zero gravity, under water, and in superhot or supercold temperatures, and it will perform all these feats even after lying around for ninety-nine years. How do they know about that ninety-nine-year promise? I haven't got ninety-nine years to wait around to test its longevity, and I've never had the urge to write upside down the way so many left-handed people do, or under water for that matter. Floating around in zero gravity is becoming more popular, but not for me. Please save that $19.95 for your favorite charity.

Next item is the solar-powered ventilated golf cap. We know that many golfers are addicted to golf gadgets and don't want to hear that it is possible to play the game without golden tees, monogrammed golf balls, calculators, and canary-colored slacks. But I don't know any golfer who, even at the modest price of $29.95, feels naked without this cap, the only one with a built-in solar-powered fan that directs a constant breeze toward your forehead. It is powered by six-and-a-half volt solar cells for daytime and two AA batteries (included!) for nightime. Does the proud owner really play golf at night, or is he so enamored of his special cap that he wears it to bed in the summer?

If tennis is your sport, how about a tennis tutor that throws 150 balls to you at speeds from ten to fifty-five miles per hour? It's only two cubic feet in size, and the battery charger is included. It should be if they expect you to pay from $879 to $1,099 for it. For a thousand dollars I'm sure I could dig up a friend to serve me a lot of shots.

Perhaps you are a birder and hope that Santa Claus will tuck a Directional Sound Amplifier in your stocking. You can attach it to your binoculars, and it will amplify faint bird calls for $54.75. I'd be more interested in a sound modifier that could tune out rock music, traffic noises, and sonic booms.

If you have been playing all this golf and tennis and tramping through the woods on bird walks to trim your waistline, you can check your progress with their talking scale. It announces your weight "in a clear, digitally synthesized voice and then (if you wish) tells you how much you have gained or lost since your last weighing." It automatically shuts off after telling you either "Have a nice day" or "Good-bye." Memory buttons allow five family members to keep track, and there is even a guest button with no memory function. Last, it will accuse "Overload!" if your weight exceeds 287 pounds.

I'm not sure my guests want the world to know how much they weigh. I doubt if we have any friends who weigh more than 287 pounds, but if we did, I'm sure that would be the last time they darkened our door with their large shadow.

If you don't get your exercise through any of these activities and are happy to stay at home with your cat, H and S has just the thing for you—an electronic cat door for $149.90 that is opened exclusively by a specially coded key worn on your cat's collar so that only *your* cat can pass through this portal. No strays, no amorous tomcats who might have followed your feline home. The password is an electrical impulse known only to you and your cat's collar. Now, that's exclusive enough for a royal Egyptian cat goddess, but I'm sure that a catnip mouse in his Christmas sock would elicit just as loud a purr from your pet on Christmas morning.

Now let us consider the Schmeckenbecker Putter. It has a built-in compass to help you find your way out of the rough; a candle to illuminate the eighteenth hole after dark; a rabbit's foot for luck; a level to help you read greens; a forty-inch tape measure to eliminate arguments over "gimme" putts; and an air horn to command silence or to speed up slow golfers. Thank God they have a sense of humor. I was beginning to worry about them, but I can tell you right now that I'm not going to pay $39.95 for it!

The Other Black Hole

All that talk about black holes in outer space reminds me of one right here on this planet. In fact, although I can't see it, it is right in our house. If we move, it travels with us. Its magnetic force attracts and swallows up George's single black sock, a shopping list, and the one book you are look-ing for. Within the last few days, two books—*The Golden Bough* and Strunk and White's *Elements of Style*—have slid into that mysterious abyss. Now, both of us *knew* that *The Golden Bough* was in the wall bookcase upstairs. We had seen it there. No more. And why Strunk and E. B. White were lured into its depths, I have no idea. I don't remember anyone borrowing it. Could we have left it in Kansas when we parted with several hundred books?

That was the first time we didn't take all our books with us when we moved. Coincidentally, it was also the first time our moving expenses were not paid by a university. Books are heavy, and you pay by the weight. So in the interest of economy, we winnowed out all the books that we thought we would never read or refer to again. But if *The Golden Bough* stayed in Kansas, why do both of us recall seeing it here in Jericho?

That is the insidious modus operandi of the Black Hole. It creates optical illusions. You are sure you put two socks in the washer, but you take out only one. You know there were several twenty-five-cent stamps in the desk drawer yesterday, but today there are only those old fourteen-cent ones that won't send your postcards on their way until you remember to buy one-cent ones.

Every time we have moved, the Black Hole has kept something as a souvenir of our residence. When we left South Burlington for Weston, Massachusetts, we realized after a few weeks that our copper boiler was no longer with us. The family that bought our house in South Burlington didn't claim it. What was the Black Hole planning to do with it—brew some black magic?

When we left Mission Hills, Kansas, to return to Vermont, we thought our hand-forged eagle, made for us by Sam Ogden of Landgrove, was returning with us. Did it ever show its beak again in Vermont? It did not, but unfortunately, we didn't realize our loss until the claim period had expired. I can't believe the movers had any interest in the eagle. The Black Hole had struck again.

Once in a while the Black Hole rejects something that it finds it didn't want after all. We have a brown towel that never belonged to us or to any of our friends. I found it lying on the grass, and its identity has remained a mystery. But a more sinister cast-off was a small black box that literally fell out of the blue onto our driveway. It contained small copper strips, and according to my husband, they could have been used to confuse a radar instrument if they had been scattered out of a plane. I think the Black Hole sucked it up and then spewed it out in disgust at man's interference with the atmosphere.

The average man accuses his wife of collaboration with the Black Hole. The cry of "What did you do with my Phillips screwdriver, my Irish tweed cap, my black cummerbund?" is heard in every household across the land. Inasmuch as I have never coveted any one of the above items, I refuse to be equated with the powers of darkness. Of course, this turns out to benefit the man of the house, because when I burrow through his bureau drawers, the closets, and the workshop, I usually find at least one of the missing articles.

But what about all the other items that have vanished over the years? Don't tell me the washing machine ate one sock at a time, or that a crow pulled the belt to my pink dress off the clothesline. My Irish grandmother would have winked and blamed it on the little people, but I know it was the Black Hole.

A State of Mind

Age may be a state of mind, but I am beginning to discover it is usually someone else's state of mind. When my mother was sixty-eight, I thought she was very old. She didn't. When I was sixty-eight, my grandson Patrick asked me how old I was. When I told him, he thought I was lucky to be that old. At six, he could hardly wait for each birthday because to him getting older meant getting nearer to being grown-up. At his tenth birthday he was so happy to at last have a two-figure age.

That may be true in the early years, but it is obvious that age is not generally revered in our culture. I have a friend, Faith Lindley, in Barre who is one hundred and two. She says that your perception of age is a case of mind over matter. If you don't mind, it doesn't matter. She is an exception because her mind is so keen that even at such an advanced age, she is surrounded by admiration.

Maybe one has earned that at one hundred and two, but I first began to doubt the pleasures of aging when I was half that age. After a talk I gave at Tufts to medical-student wives based on my book *How To Be a Doctor's Wife Without Really Dying,* one of the young women came up and said, "I don't see how anyone as *old* as you could know how we feel!" She meant it as a compliment. Most remarks about age are meant that way, but they don't always fall gently on the recipient's ear. When I tell someone my age, they often say, "you don't look it." But what I hear is the "it" which means "*that* old," or as my father used to say, "One foot in the grave and the other on a banana peel."

I met a recent graduate of Mount Holyoke who knew that it was also my college, and she asked what class I had been in. When I said 1936, she gasped, "Oh my, that was thirty years before I was *born*! What was the college like then? Did you have cars and radios?" True, we didn't have TV or computers, but neither did we have drugs or AIDS or atom bombs. It was the kinder, gentler world that George Bush dreams about.

I find that family roles are beginning to be reversed nowadays. I used to be the caretaker. Now Patty and Debbie are becoming protective of us, offering to help with lugging hundred-pound grain bags, mowing the lawn, and shoveling snow. I've always been happy at any age to accept help with chores I don't especially enjoy, but I notice that George balks at the implication that he needs help. The old refrain, "Please mother, I want to do it myself" is now spoken by the father, not by the child.

The years are long in childhood. When you are ten, twenty seems old. When you are thirty, sixty is old. But when you are seventy, you are not thinking in terms of one hundred and forty! But you do shove it ahead—maybe into the late eighties.

Like beauty, age is in the eye of the beholder. Unfortunately, they are not synonymous, but at least one can aspire to dignity if not charm.

Born Too Early

I'm an alien in this world of computers. I almost said "computerized world," but I don't like to see nouns pretending to be verbs. I'm not "maximizing" my protests, I'm emphasizing them, and computers are not "impacting" on me, they are making an impact on my peaceful Stone Age way of life.

It takes me half an hour to decipher the efficient-looking printout we receive from our stockbroker. Our "simplified" tax form terrifies me. Why do television producers think the average viewer is a moron while the tax people assume we are fiscal wizards? George has been involved in the practice of medicine and medical administration for most of his life, but the ubiquitous "this is not a bill" from Blue Cross–Blue Shield does a good job of concealing its message from him. He knows the medical terminology, but they don't speak in that tongue. They speak in symbols and initials.

Answering machines render me tongue-tied — a condition

my family will tell you is not normal for me. My friends imply that because I write in longhand on a yellow legal pad and then type these pieces, I am overdue for a word processor. I *do* use an electric typewriter, but even that gets away from me and occasionally prints a letter twice because my finger rested longer on the key than the typewriter thought it should. They extol its speed and dexterity in rewriting and moving paragraphs around. I have a quaint notion that you should think out what you are going to say before you write and that rewriting something three times is like reheating the lamb roast three nights in a row. All right, maybe certain soups and stews improve with reheating, but not light essays.

Now, I don't want to regress to the point of cranking a car. In fact, I was born a little too late to have ever done that, but as a child I watched my father sprain his wrist and his disposition doing it. And I don't want to have to poke a little needle around on a crystal set to get sound out of a radio. I even enjoy the remote control on the TV, but mostly for muting the screamers and commercials.

Our washing machine is a great improvement over the set tubs and wringers of my childhood, and I love the way it goes about its business independently. I even admire the way it protests loudly and screeches to a halt when it becomes unbalanced from an overload. We should all have that luxury.

An automatic garage-door opener looks great even though it seems like black magic, but last week our neighbor's automatic opener froze closed, and it took him an hour to open the door. Automatic car-window openers can have their balky moments too. I saw one that froze shut at a toll booth,

and the driver had to get out of the car to pay the toll. I haven't felt lonesome enough to want a talking car, although the voice in Jack Cross's Chrysler New Yorker is a mellifluous baritone gently reminding him that the gas is low or a seatbelt unfastened. It is polite too, thanking Jack every time he fulfills its modest requests.

Am I the only one who pictures a little teller running around minting the crisp new bills at the automatic teller at the bank? I know he's in there. I can hear his little feet!

But I am troubled by the fact that my grandsons have never wound a watch or heard the tick-tock of a clock. In fact, they wouldn't be able to tell time if their parents hadn't told them about the big hand and the little hand, as old-fashioned as the birds and the bees. I think kids should know how to tie shoelaces and shift gears. Living in the north country, we find that manual shift is an advantage in maneuvering a car out of a drift at our will rather than the car's.

My grandsons have never seen a running board (the hem of my coat would be a lot cleaner if we had them), an inner tube, real Christmas tree candles, or an iceman. They've never seen an electric car either, though that may be in their future. The one I used to see humming around the streets of Montclair at a *very* low speed wouldn't be much use for a long trip, but it didn't pollute the air. They get along fine without these outmoded things, and they don't miss some good things they never had, like two-cent stamps, five-cent bus fares, mail delivered twice a day, and department stores that delivered.

All I ask is for them to let me live happily without an answering machine, a word processor, or a table at a restaurant with a fax. You didn't know I knew that one, did you?

The Sixth Sense
of Christmas

Christmas in Vermont looks as if it were painted by Grandma Moses, which it often was. It smells like a bakery in a pine forest, tastes like a rerun of Thanksgiving plus plum pudding, sounds like stamping feet and Christmas carols, and feels like the North Pole. There is all the snow you could ask for on evergreen boughs and ski slopes, and quite a bit more than you asked for on your windshield and driveway. The white church in each village is lit by a floodlight tucked in the bushes so that it shines out over the village green like a benediction. On the church door there is a large wreath of greens from the nearby woods, and one candle glows from each window.

But this, you say, could be true of Christmas anywhere in the Northeast or points west that were settled by New Englanders. Yes, but you see, Christmas is such an intensely personal experience that I can only describe it as it has happened to me, and I find myself most often remembering our Christmases in Vermont, not only with the usual five senses but with the sixth sense of Christmas—the wonder and delight in little kindnesses, the almost unbearable excitement of childhood, and the recurring hope for peace and goodwill.

How loyally we cling to our heritage of Christmas patterns! The Christmas tree, for me, has to be not only natural but really should be balsam or spruce. It should not be flocked, made out of plastic, or tinted an unnatural green. Its lights should not blink on and off like a movie marquee. It should be set up just before Christmas and remain up at least until after New Year's Day, the longer the better, which is a hangover from my childhood reluctance to relinquish the look and smell of Christmas in the house. Most of its ornaments should have been in the family for years, with only an occasional addition to replace the ones that got juggled too vigorously or sat upon. The ornaments are treasured because they are beautiful or because they were made by the children or simply because they are old friends with whom we have shared the bittersweet moments of many Christmases.

During all the long years of my childhood, at each Christmas we walked down the street to see the Mullers' Christmas tree. They were a somber, rather isolated German family who had become more so during World War I. Their grown sons and daughter never married, and all lived at home. But at Christmas, the gaiety of Christmases past in Germany burst through the bonds of their reserve. They set up an enormous tree in the front hall. It touched the ceiling and gave the appearance of piercing it because several feet of the top of it had been lopped off to make it fit. Gauzy birds circled rococo angels with spun-glass wings. The lower branches were as big around as the trunk of our tree. They had to be to support five, huge, colored metallic balls, the size of bowling balls but twice as heavy. I have never seen balls like these anywhere since. Mrs. Muller had brought them from her parents' home in Germany, and they were very old, sapphire blue, deep ruby, emerald green, silver and gold. I never see real jewels without thinking of the Mullers' Christmas tree. I was allowed to lift them gently to marvel at their weight and wonder at my Lilliputian reflection on their shiny surface. Each year Mrs. Muller gave us a box of German cookies, *Springerle* and some that were as hard as rocks with a glazed white frosting – not my favorites but one of the memorable tastes of Christmas.

When I was seven, we lived in Geneva, Switzerland, and there were new tastes that meant Christmas: marzipan shaped into brightly colored fruits and vegetables, the bland smoky taste of roasted chestnuts, and wonderful hunks of semisweet chocolate that we carried to school to eat with French bread at recess.

Christmas in Europe then was filled with seasonal sounds unfamiliar to an American child, many more church bells in a variety of tones, street vendors, and street singers. Greetings of *Joyeux Noël* and *Grüss Gott* were intensified by the crystalline air. But even New York sounds different at Christmas. People laugh more, Salvation Army bell-ringers are at every corner, and the great cavern of Grand Central Station is filled with amplified Christmas carols. But what I miss in the city is the near silence in Vermont on Christmas Eve, when we look across the snowy fields, moonlit, motionless, as though the whole world were waiting for Christmas morning.

The smells of Christmas should also be old friends – the

turkey, a fragrant curl of steam from the slit in the mince pie, or a suet pudding made from an old Vermont rule, celery, onion, sage, all the smells that make the description of the Cratchits' Christmas dinner the best part of *A Christmas Carol*. In fact I never cared for Scrooge or the ghosts at all. And of course, throughout the house the fragrance of pine or balsam or spruce.

The feel of Christmas in Vermont is full of sharp contrasts. Of course it is cold, cold enough to delight in the enveloping warmth of coming indoors. A warm house on a warm day is nothing. A warm house when the thermometer slinks down below zero is an affirmation of life to be grateful for.

The tree is prickly to the touch, but it doesn't stab you viciously like the Scotch pines we had in Kansas. Like most of us, its needles lie smooth if they aren't rubbed the wrong way. A warm cheek is pressed against your cold one, and the heat of the old rosy bricks on the hearth seeps through the wool of your socks.

But against the backdrop of all these tastes and sounds and smells, the memorable moments that distinguish one Christmas from another are always simple things, the unexpected homemade gifts, the felt placemats Debbie made for me on the plane while she was flying home from New York to Kansas City, the paper airplane in the shape of the one in which George learned to fly that Patty made and filled with George's favorite chocolate candy kisses in piñata fashion, the enormous bag of golf tees, the red mittens that Mrs. McClure, a little elderly neighbor lady in Jericho, knit for me one winter because she thought after so much city living I might not have warm country gloves.

They cannot be bought. They can only be given, true Christmas gifts because they are a part of the giver's life and

love, just as the birth of Christ symbolizes the worth of each individual. It is the awareness, even if we feel it only once a year, that love and kindness can still save the world.

Visions of sugar plums, talking dolls, or nintendos may dance through the heads of the young, but it is this sense of hope and yearning and wonder that is the sixth sense of Christmas.

Winter Blues

There are two kinds of winter blues. One is cabin fever, more properly called the winter blahs, that all of us semi-hibernators in the north country skid into once in a while between November and March. The other winter blues are visible on any sunny day when the ground is snow-covered. The snow is likely to be with us from Thanksgiving till Easter. The sun is more occasional. Blue is not the dominant color on gray or snowy days, when the lacy silhouette of dark branches against pale skies is varied only by dark-green evergreens, red barns, and the occasional brick house.

But on a clear blue and gold day, the sky is a dome of ombre blues, delphinium blue at the zenith, shading to the fragile pastel of bluets at the horizon. On the snowy landscape as the short day hurries toward night, lengthening blue shadows stretch out from every tree and snowdrift and, in fact, from every elevation from a blade of dry grass to a towering silo. These blues are muted-thundercloud blue. Along the highway or anywhere where a cliff wears an overhang of ice, the color is iceblue, pale, translucent aquamarine like the inside of a glacier. The fields are suffused with a wash of grayblue and even the evergreens look navy blue.

Just before the sun sinks behind the Adirondacks, a burst of light seems to illuminate the western side of Mount Mansfield and Camel's Hump, turning the snow-covered slopes the tender shell pink of the inside of a conch shell. The delicate color lasts only a few minutes and deepens to rose, mauve, and deep purple.

Twilight settles over the villages and countryside with the color and bloom of blueberries and mutes the other colors until even the white farmhouses and church steeples are Wedgewood blue, only pricked here and there with the yellow glow of lights winking on in houses and barns.

In this soft indigo twilight, white curls of smoke reach up from chimneys, and the golden fingers of light from kitchen windows beckon children and workers home. Their footsteps crunch on the icy gray-blue paths, and they walk more quickly in anticipation of the warmth and fragrance of wood fires, a savory stew simmering, and something fruity and cinnamony in the oven.

High in the darkened sky a white moon, serene and cold, rides through the waves of clouds like a galleon on an infinite sea of midnight blue.

Time Remembered

When you are very young, the long years stretch out into infinity. You live entirely in the present or in the immediate future. The past has no reality because you can't identify with a world so different from your own. Our grandsons can't imagine a world without TV or OP's. At their age, I couldn't imagine a world without telephones or radios, but I liked the stories my parents told me about their childhoods. Of course they had the unreality of fairy tales, but they gave me the same pleasurable excitement.

When you reach threescore and ten, you find that remembrance of things past sometimes has more poignancy than the present. The clarity of detail with which you remember your eighth birthday party is sharper than your memory of the dinner party you attended last week. And the sensory impressions of summer hegiras in the Twenties are more acutely recalled than your last vacation.

The Roaring Twenties

Everything was noisy in the twenties—the first electric iceboxes, the radio with a loudspeaker instead of earphones, and our first monstrosity of a car. If my father had taken two driving lessons instead of one before he applied for his driver's license, there might have been less roaring every time he shifted gears. There were no road tests. You just read the rules and asked for a license. No one could have accused him of riding the clutch.

Having touched it gingerly with his toe, he drew back his foot and tried to force the gears into the next position. Eventually, he had to enlist further aid from the clutch, unwillingly and with the accompanying roar of the engine as he raced the motor to maintain his supremacy.

I doubt if it intimidated the car, but it certainly scared me. The car sickness that harassed me on trips from New Jersey to Maine was induced by lack of equanimity more than by lack of equilibrium, and there was more than enough fresh air in a Studebaker touring car.

Nothing less than a hurricane brought the isinglass curtains out of hiding. In the first place, no one could ever remember where they were, so the passengers had to climb out in the rain while the seats were removed—along with the skin from several knuckles. The effort wasn't wasted. Two left-handed gloves, a Harding-Coolidge button, and a battered copy of *The Youth's Companion* nestled in the dusty cavern. Even when the curtains were found, they had always shrunk in some mysterious way so that no amount of yanking would stretch the snaps to reach the little metal knobs intended for them. But the milling and moiling and twisting helped everyone forget the rain, and I don't remember ever being carsick during a storm.

This was the lost generation, all right. We had no doubts about our destination. Whether it was world peace or the summer cottage, we knew exactly where we were going. But in both cases we got lost along the way.

We didn't just take a trip. Traveling was so uncomfortable that we needed at least a month's vacation to build up our strength for the return journey. The nearest thing to those trips in our own children's experience was *Wagon Train* on television.

Packing the car was a solemn rite performed by Father. Anyone might carry out the suitcases, the duffel bag, the wicker case full of bedding, or the Thermos bottle that rattled, but only Father arranged the baggage, and it was advisable not to offer suggestions. In theory all the luggage was confined to a folding metal baggage rack on the running board. Of course, when this was packed, you couldn't get out of the car on the right-hand side, a fact that was frequently forgotten by children. The door opened easily but only an inch, and it required superhuman strength to shut it again. Somehow only half the luggage would fit into the rack. The rest was stowed, tucked, or jammed under your feet, between your knees, and finally in your lap. As the smallest in the family, I was always assigned the most cramped corner, where I bent one leg around the brown tarpaulin roll-up, ducked my head under the fishing pole, and held the lunch on my lap. The only unfilled lap was Father's. He needed freedom of movement to drive the car. He could have used a lot of other things, too, like mechanical aptitude and a more intimate acquaintance with the driver's manual, but elbow room was the only requirement he recognized. Mother settled herself, rigid and smiling, at his side, clutching the Blue Book in one gloved hand and a bottle of Bel-Ans for me in the other.

When we were all pinioned to our post, and Mother had reassured herself three times that the gas was turned off and the window over the cellar door locked, Father cranked the car and leaped from the crank to the gas and spark levers on the steering wheel, and the car trembled and began to have convulsions. The neighbors waved and shouted gaily in mock envy—and then the engine died. Father's frustration and Mother's forced cheerfulness waxed and the neighbors' enthusiasm waned as we ran through the overture again. At last father tamed the wild beast into submission, and we roared out of the driveway, setting our determined faces northward.

The first half hour was familiar and required no consultations with the Blue Book. But after that, the trackless wastes lay in wait for our caravan. If there were road maps, they must have been used only for geodetic surveys and bore no similarity to the trail we blazed. Highways were "routes," pronounced *routs*—quite appropriately. They had no numbers, although a few bore titles such as the Boston Post Road, Jacob's Ladder, and the Mohawk Trail, reminiscent of their romantic past and descriptive of their present condition. As we drove past Albert Payson Terhune's estate in northern New Jersey, nearly dislocating our necks trying to get a glimpse of Lad, Mother started her literary guided tour, with frequent interruptions when the Blue Book called her back to her post as navigator and co-pilot.

"Goodness, Charles, we should have turned right at the four corners in Tarrytown instead of talking about Washington Irving and Sunnyside. But I didn't want the girls to miss Sunnyside."

The girls would have preferred missing Sunnyside to missing the road. My sister began sniffling, the first symptom of impending misery over becoming lost. She matched every wave of my nausea with anxiety over being lost in a city. What fate she dreaded, I could only dimly imagine. She was four years older than I and an omnivorous reader, so I assumed that her vicarious experiences had made her familiar with the underworld in Danbury or Pittsfield. My own imagination was even more fertile than her fears. She was simply scared to death of traffic because it completely unnerved father and plunged us all into gloomy silence.

When mother ran short of literary landmarks, historical and political allusions were substituted. She considered it a personal favor that Coolidge had been at his father's house in Plymouth, Vermont, on the night of August 2 when he acceded to the presidency, because it was no trouble at all to go through Plymouth on the way home. No trouble—except that the engine became overheated on the steep hill and we had to stop and rush around back to put large rocks behind the wheels so that we wouldn't end up in Echo Lake. Fortunately rocks are as plentiful as hills in Vermont; and, while the engine hissed and gurgled, I waded in the brook and gathered blue chicory, starting a full-time romance with my adopted state.

Colonel John Coolidge graciously showed us the spot where he had administered the oath of office to his taciturn son. The stopover was memorable to me because Mother, intoxicated by our proximity to the father of the President, let me spend a dollar for one of the whittled canes that Colonel Coolidge was turning out rapidly between tourists and chores.

We didn't explore the byways of Vermont very often. In spite of the charm of the villages and the dignity of the Green Mountains, the early tourist dreaded those rutted roads. Following a car was such a choking, blinding experience that father would accelerate the motor as much as he could, "ah-oo-gah" the horn wildly, and squeeze past the offending dust cloud, our faces whipped by the branches of the birch trees that bordered the narrow road. Luckily, there were few cars on the road. In fact, a New Jersey car in New England was such a novelty that when we came upon another one, the occupants of both cars honked and waved and drove on, warmed by the encounter with fellow adventurers.

From midafternoon, Mother's nesting urge prompted her to think aloud about a suitable place to spend the night. The Blue Book recommended hotels and inns, but Father, used to traveling around the world alone, could never adjust to the fact that food and lodging for four cost so much more than it did for one. He tried to trim expenses by avoiding anything resembling a resort or hotel. We patronized the frame houses at the edges of towns with "Tourists Accommodated" signs. Father was more than willing to stop if they also clearly specified "$1.00 per person." If they didn't, we would draw up under the elms, case the house for any undesirable characteristics, and delegate Mother to go in and inquire. She was always invited to inspect the rooms, which she did in a perfunctory way while we waited outside with bated breath until she reappeared on the gingerbread encrusted porch and waved her approval over the syringa bushes.

Mother never decided against a tourist home. I'm sure she would have considered that as rude as criticizing the guest room in a friend's house. Both she and the lady of the house performed the ritual with apprehension but emerged radiant and blessed by mutual approval. Bedraggled and dusty, we straggled past the man of the house, who sat in the parlor, only his shirtsleeves, caught up in elastic bands, protruding from the evening paper. We were shown into clean, impersonal rooms that had been stripped of the trappings of their former tenants. But as though reluctant to be disinherited by those it had sheltered, each room had some subtle hint of its owner's personality. Sometimes it was a pennant from Williston Academy on the wall, left in place lest its removal reveal the faded condition of the rest of the wallpaper. There might be a dress form in the back of the deep closet, or a dried-up corsage of roses left in the bureau drawer to impart its faded whisper of romance.

I was always conscious of the ghosts of the sons and daughters who had married and bequeathed those rooms to us, and a vague sense of trespassing augmented the discomfort of the brass bed with a hollow in the middle of the mattress. My small uprooted spirit wilted during the annual transplantation, and I fell asleep yearning for my recently abandoned tree house or the geniality of the hay-scented barn waiting for me in Maine.

Misgivings about the engine's ability to conquer every mountain convinced my father that we should follow the Connecticut valley. My sister was assured that we would be far west of Boston, and mother remembered happily that Emily Dickinson's house was waiting for us in Amherst.

As we inched along beside the campus looking for this literary landmark, Father muttered that even in death Emily Dickinson withdrew from the public eye, and wouldn't Mother settle for a dinosaur track near Northampton, where there was little danger of encountering unsociable descendants?

The Deerfield Massacre was never as real to me as the Battle of Bennington, in spite of the fact that I had an ancestor who fought at Deerfield. Maybe if the outcome had been more favorable, the family lore would have made more of his efforts. But I could identify with the children of Bennington scurrying up the steep stairs to strip their bedsteads of rope to secure the British prisoners and gathering lead from house to house to be melted into bullets on that humid August day in 1776.

Once we crossed the Maine border, a sense of victory mellowed the family climate as much as the late June sun and the creaking of redwinged blackbirds in the meadows.

Haying had not started, and the tall grass was silvered by the wind like squalls on Lake Champlain. Even another flat tire and the long wait while Father patched the tube and pumped it back up by hand meant only a welcome excursion into the fields for the first tiny fragrant wild strawberries.

Our excitement mounted as we caught the first glimpse of the Kennebec River, clogged with logs above the pulp mill at Waterville. I began to wriggle my feet out of the brown Coward oxfords that would be closeted during the weeks ahead. The car sickness, the flat tires, the overheated engine, and the unintentional detours were sloughed off with my shoes. While mother quoted appropriate passages concerning hills from both the 121st Psalm and Ethan Allen, Father glanced back at our bulging disheveled caravan.

"Who said we couldn't get here from there?" he sang out proudly. "*Deus vult*, we made it again!"

Blizzards and Tornados

When our grandsons ask me about "the olden days," they aren't thinking about World War I or even World War II. To them, anything that happened before they were born is hidden under a veil of antiquity. I can remember feeling the same way about the suffragettes and the Kaiser.

What I really want to tell them are stories that my mother and father told me because there is no one else now living who could tell them about their great-grandmother's life in the 1880s in South Dakota. My mother was born in 1880 in Harlan, Iowa, but they moved to South Dakota in 1888. Remember the blizzard of '88? She did. They didn't live in a sod hut out on the prairie. They lived in a frame house quite near town because my grandfather was a banker, a newspaper editor, and a schoolteacher at various times. With a small population—this was before South Dakota became a state—an educated man wore several hats. He probably carried a cane, too, as befitted a respected citizen. The children went to a one-room schoolhouse some distance from their homes. As you've been told ad nauseam, everybody walked a mile or more to school in those days. As a matter of fact, I walked more than a mile to school and back four times a day in the 1920s in Montclair, New Jersey. My grandsons think I was lucky never to have ridden a school bus in my life. They would prefer to scuff home through the falling leaves in autumn, dodge all the worms on the sidewalks after a spring rain, or have snowball fights on the way home, as we did.

As my mother told it, on that March morning in 1888, it had been snowing for some time, and the drifts were piling up around the school. The children were delighted. They couldn't even see the outhouse. Shortly after noon, two of the fathers came to the school with long coils of clothesline. The children were bundled into their coats, lined up, and tied around their waists until they resembled a human string of beads. One father led the littlest first child, and the other father walked at the other end of the line to rescue any stumblers. It was a lot of fun. The children giggled as they wallowed through the blinding snow to the nearest house. There they were unwrapped, warmed by the fire, ate supper, and spent the night wall-to-wall children on the kitchen floor. What a picnic for an eight-year-old and fifteen other children from first to sixth grade! My mother's older brother Lee was ten, her sister Sue was six. Three from one family, so it is not surprising that her father was the rearguard.

The prairie winters were harsh, but when spring came, they faced another weather hazard—tornados. Every rural home had a storm cellar. There were no weather warnings on the radios. There were no radios, no telephones, no

automobiles. I don't think our grandsons can imagine life without phone or TV, any more than I have experienced whale-oil lamps or making a fire with tinder and sparks. My grandparents had a tornado cellar out in the field beyond their house and barn. It was used primarily as a root cellar for storing potatoes, onions, beets and carrots. It looked like a low mound with a wooden door. There were no windows and no light once you shut the door.

My mother told me that one unseasonably warm day in spring, the air was heavy and still. No birds sang. The sky looked dirty yellow, and far away they heard a faint roar like a train in the distance. My grandfather rushed home from town in his buggy, put the horse in the barn, and ran to the house.

94

"Get into the storm cellar!" he shouted, "Get all the children. Run! It's coming this way!"

My grandmother, still in her apron, handed baby Jack to my mother, grabbed little Will and Edith by the hands, and shooed the older children, Sue and Lee and my mother Daisy, ahead of her. They had to yank on the heavy wooden door. It creaked open, and they scrambled in, falling over boxes and baskets. My grandfather was last and pulled the door shut behind him. There they crouched in the pitch dark while the roaring came louder and nearer. They could hear things banging around outside. After a while it was very still, and grandfather shoved the door open. Their house was still standing! So was the barn, but their windmill had disappeared—just gone, never found. My mother's most vivid memory was that two of their chickens were running around, squawking wildly with all their feathers gone, picked clean but very much alive.

Nothin' But a Hawk

My father grew up on a farm in Michigan. Life was not easy for farm boys a hundred years ago. They were expected to do the chores and work in the fields after school. There was sugaring in March, planting in April and May, and hoeing and harvesting all summer and fall. But he also had some happy memories, and for the rest of his life he had the farmer's awareness of signs and portents of changes in the weather and took delight in a small vegetable garden. His mother was so determined that her three children would get an education that she moved into Ann Arbor for five years so that they could go to the University of Michigan. Grandpa stayed on the farm and provided them with most of their food.

Money was scarce in my father's boyhood. His proudest possessions were a rifle and a pet ferret. When he could be spared from farm chores, particularly in the fall, he patrolled the woods, sending his ferret down rabbit holes or stalking crows and hawks. When I was about ten, the same age he was when he got his rifle, he used to sit on the side of my bed at night and tell me stories about his boyhood. One story I asked for over and over again, until I knew it by heart.

"The day after I got my gun, I hurried home from school, put an apple in my pocket, picked up my gun, and started off across the field for the woods. It was early fall, and the corn stubble was rough under my bare feet. I would try to step over the rows, but I was in too much of a hurry to be careful. In the woods the maple leaves were beginning to fall, and the walking was soft and moist on the gold and scarlet leaves. Once in a while a twig snapped or a squirrel chattered, but everything else was still. There were no cars then, no airplanes. Even the train was miles away, and you could hear the mournful whistle only if the wind was from the south. Nobody told me what to do or what not to do. It was very peaceful. The woods belonged to me. The sky was deep blue with a few popcorn clouds, and at the top of a dead elm tree I saw a hawk. He was watching the field, looking for mice. His back was turned to me, but that didn't mean he couldn't see almost all the way around.

"I crept toward the elm as slowly as I could, trying to stay behind the big maple trunks and making as little noise as possible. When I was within range of the tree, I slowly raised my rifle, squinted through the sight, and *bang!* scared myself out of my wits. The hawk dropped like a stone, and I tore to the foot of the tree. There he lay on his back, his talons clenched and his eyes flashing. I picked up a stick and hit him over the head. *Thass!* Dead! With my heart pounding, I picked him up by the feet and raced home galloping into the yard and leaping up the kitchen steps. My mother came to the kitchen door wiping her hands on her apron.

"'Why, Charlie boy, what *have* you got?'

"I was short of breath, bursting with pride and very near to tears. My older brother was looking over my mother's shoulder.

"I swallowed the lump in my throat and said, 'Oh, nothin' but a hawk.'"

Box Socials

I have never been to a box social. In my childhood we had church suppers, strawberry festivals, and an annual ladies' frenzy called the Christmas bazaar, but no box socials. My knowledge of them comes solely from the bedtime stories my father told me. Any similarity between the box socials he experienced and the ones he described to me was purely coincidental.

According to him, every lady of the congregation packed up a picnic lunch for two in a shoebox, decorated it according to her fancy, and added it to the pile on the auctioneer's table. A young girl might drop a hint to the sister of the young man she had her eye on about the color of the crepe paper or ribbon adorning her box, but otherwise both the contents and the donor were dark secrets.

Then the boxes would be auctioned off, and each young man would bid for his girlfriend's box. If he won the box, he also won the honor of sitting with her and sharing the contents. The way my father told it, the boxes were works of art rivaling Fabergé eggs in ornamentation, resplendent in lavender ribbons, gold braid, and artificial flowers from last year's Easter bonnet. And what contents! The actual homemade bread and butter sandwiches filled with ham or cheese and the deviled eggs and the molasses cookies were transformed into ambrosia if made by your best girl. My father went a step farther and imagined concoctions wild enough to send me into squirms of horror or delight.

He told me that a box wrapped in black paper and adorned with a skull and crossbones might contain porcupine quills, a squashed toad, and a discarded snakeskin, as well as foods he knew I didn't like—cold oatmeal, turnips, and tapioca pudding. When I would plead for mercy, he pretended to pick up and open a blue velvet box trimmed with silver ribbon and sequin stars with the most improbable contents he could think up.

Vichyssoise (which I had never tasted), peacock tongues, pomegranate seeds, cherries jubilee, chocolate ice cream sodas, and my eight-year-old idea of heavenly fare—lemon meringue pie. Visions of these delights danced through my head as I drifted off to sleep.

A skinny little girl still wearing oatmeal-colored Dr. Denton's with feet snuggled under the covers while her tall, even skinnier father in a dark business suit with a celluloid collar, smelling of the Erie Railroad he rode every day from Montclair to Hoboken, sat on the edge of the bed and slipped back into memories of his boyhood.

My mother felt that cooking was a burden that had been thrust upon her by the disappearance of live-in domestic help. Had men-of-the-house been welcome in kitchens in those days, my father might have been a creative cook. It never occurred to him, except to pop corn on Sunday nights, but he expressed his interest in food by bringing home oysters, shrimp, a fresh coconut, a pineapple, or an avocado from the Washington Market in New York, and in rolling such exotic names as *sukiyaki* and *mulligatawny* off his tongue as he told me about the box socials in Tecumseh, Michigan.

Ghosts in the Attic

One of the interesting items we found between the joists in our attic in South Burlington was a notebook containing the inventory of the contents of our house at the time of the owner John Fay's death in 1809. A side saddle, feather beds, bedsteads and cords, candle stands, potash kittles (sic), and a chafin dish (sic) describe life in early Vermont better than a history book. But what was of special interest to me was the penciled first draft of a letter, written at least forty years after the inventory was compiled, on the blank pages of the book. The letter was written by eleven-year-old Lissie Fay to her older brother Fred in California. Fred had been lured west by the gold rush, which must have seemed very exotic to Lizzie in Vermont.

She wrote, "My dearest brother. You cannot begin to calculate how much pleasure we derived from reading your most *excellent* letters which we received today. There were two letters, one of them we should have received last weak [sic] but did not therefore you must know we had a regular

feast, the best we have had for a long time. Your last letter
was very good but you said you had a sore hand which we
have thought a great deal about fearing it might be something cerious [sic]. In time we rejoyced [sic] to hear that it
was well. You did not mention it therefore we concluded
that you would have no more trouble with it. I fear, dear
brother that you write only the bright side. Is that the way
you did? I think you do not tell how tired you are when
you get to your cottage at night then have to get your own
supper. I wish almost that I were there to help you make
cake. If we broke the spoons we would just hide them in

the wall. Dear brother do you not think about that often? I do every day. I imagine you gents look rather funny cooking your victuals. Oh how I would like to be a mouse in the wall to see and hear you perform. Now if I should happen to turn into a mouse and go there you tell your friend not to shoot me. You said he was watching a mouse. I presume they are rather troublesome but I'll not be. But a truse [sic] to all badinage. Cousin Kate came here today. She is as lively as ever. She has a very ardent lover down south and we expect to lose her next fall. If you ever see R. Barstow (?) tell him that Kate's heart is not broken. I am in the parlor by the front window. Your pretty picture is here beside me. It looks so much like you it seems hardly necessary to write a letter to Cat when you are so near."

Now what did she mean about those spoons? In the inventory there was an item, "Six large silver tablespoons," which had no doubt been brought from Bennington when John Fay and Susannah were married. They were Lizzie and Fred's grandparents, so those spoons were family heirlooms. When little Lizzie was making a cake and fooling around with Fred and if she broke two of those delicate silver spoons, wouldn't her natural reaction be to hide the evidence of this heinous crime with her brother Fred's collaboration?

Our daughter Patty was also eleven when we found this notebook and the letters. She was delighted that a girl her age one hundred years before had hidden the silver spoons, and of course, she wanted to tear the layers of wallpaper off the walls and hunt for the spoons. We didn't dismantle the house, but I like to imagine that the Bennington silver tablespoons are still hidden somewhere in the wall of that house, still standing at 725 Hinesburg Road in South Burlington. Every old house should have some hidden treasure.

We Have Met the Enemy and He Is Us

"Mine! Mine! Mine!" shouts the three-year-old, glaring defiantly at a playmate who is zeroing in on his favorite toy. Territorial imperative develops early, and although most of us are coerced into modifying our behavior to fit in with societal attitudes, the more of us there are, the worse we behave. People in a crowded city are ruder and pushier than their rural cousins. Unfortunately, the city emigrants who are infiltrating the north country are bringing their aggressive and acquisitive tendencies with them. I can remember a time when, if you stalled at an intersection in South Burlington, the car behind you would wait without protest till you coaxed your engine to life. If you had a flat tire on a gravel road, the first car to come by would stop and its driver would offer to help. Country folk were more dependent on each other, and so, for the most part, they followed the Golden Rule. Now, in looking out for numero uno, we are destroying our environment, filling up our planet with toxic waste and plastic refuse, and polluting our air with acid raid. When I carry a basket or an L. L. Bean canvas tote to the supermarket, I have to argue with the checkout girl to let me use my own container. What good are all the air fresheners if the fragrant air is toxic? A gift of mail-order steak arrives sealed in a plastic pouch inside a Styrofoam cooler with dry ice inside a container twenty times the size of the product. The meat is used up promptly. The plastic and Styrofoam will remain virtually unchanged in the Jericho dump for centuries.

In Pogo's words, "We have met the enemy and he is us." And he is even uglier than we thought.

In nature the male animal is usually more territorial and aggressive than the female. The female is the nester and nurturer. But now that women are claiming equal space in the marketplace, the fire on the hearth has gone out, and we may be producing a generation of women who give activist lip-service to peace and love but who are not home long enough to rekindle the fire on that hearth and cook a meal the whole family can enjoy together.

When we say, "It's a jungle out there," we imply that nature is cruel. But animals kill for food. Man kills for sport or acquisition. On the African veldt the lion kills and eats one eland. He doesn't wipe out the whole herd the way man does with the atomic bomb or tries to with anti-Semitism.

I didn't really mean to get on a soapbox. What I was remembering as I read Pogo's words were several instances of bird behavior. At the home of Georgia Mitchum, the sculptress in Weybridge, we were sitting in her living room watching a cardinal hurl himself at the window. He didn't just fly into it blindly. Those were purposeful attacks. Over and over again, he pecked and beat his wings against the pane. Who was he attacking? His own reflection. In order to establish his claim to the territory, he felt impelled to drive away that cardinal he saw in the window. He hadn't heard about Pogo. A few years later, there was a commotion on our deck. A redstart was perched on a porch chair, looking at the window, then dive-bombing the bird he saw. He repeatedly flew at the window until he was ruffled, exhausted and gasping for breath. He would rest awhile, gathering the strength to attack the image again. He finally made me so miserable that I went out there and shooed him away to protect him from himself.

But who is going to protect us from us? Government organizations and environmental groups can't be expected to do it. Each one of us must listen to Pogo if we hope to save our world.

It's Never Too Late

In his book *All I Really Need to Know I Learned in Kindergarten*, Robert Fulghum lists some essential skills. And he is quite right. They are as fundamental as the Ten Commandments and as kind as the Golden Rule. The only problem is that we don't always follow them. Here are a few of my favorites.

Share everything. I'm not advocating communism, but have you seen the salaries of the executives of large corporations? Nobody needs an income of over a million. Donald Trump owns enough buildings to house all of New York's homeless and the street sleepers of Washington as well. He must have skipped kindergarten and started school with advanced economics. Sharing everything is a hard precept to follow because we are all naturally acquisitive to a degree. But we can share many more things than we do—knowledge, expertise, burdens, and friendship.

Put things back where you found them. If you cut down the trees, replant some. Instead of turning farmland into a mall, help the farmers stay in farming with tax benefits and decent prices for their products. If you borrow a billion dollars, pay it back. Simplistic? Of course—most sensible things are.

Clean up your own mess. Now, that doesn't apply only to milk and finger paints. We are messing up our world much faster than we are improving it. As the Third World countries become developed, they are going to add to the pollution of water, air, and land.

One of the positive steps in Vermont has been River Watch. When federal funds became available in the 1960s to help clean up rivers, Henry Bourne of Woodstock was one of the leaders in the effort to improve the quality of the Ottauquechee River, which had become, in his words, "an open sewer." Harry Goon, Woodstock's chemistry teacher, oversees the program, with local citizens and high school students measuring water temperature, taking samples, testing for bacteria, and identifying poor or nonexistent septic systems. River Watch director Jack Byrne helps groups on five rivers in the Northeast set up their own testing programs. Even though water quality is relatively high in Vermont, there is need for monitoring clarity, acidity, algae, and phosphorus as well as bacteria. If we want to be able to swim and fish in our waterways, we must go back to kindergarten and learn to clean up our mess.

That's just water. How about plastic? Disposable diapers may have improved the quality of life for young mothers, but they are overfilling our landfills. They could be made of biodegradable materials. The packaging of groceries and most of the products we buy could be greatly simplified, and the groceries could be carried home in paper bags. A few supermarkets are now offering a choice of containers. But why not carry your own tote bag, string bag, or basket, as people have done in Europe for generations?

What about cans and bottles? Recycle them. Newspapers and magazines—recycle. They are doing it in some cities, but I notice that in Brooklyn they chose Brooklyn Heights, a more affluent neighborhood, where the people are more aware of ecological problems. It's a little more work for the consumer to recycle, but are any of us so busy that we can't separate our throwaways?

I'll get down off my soapbox (wooden) and get back to another precept that Mr. Fulghum learned in kindergarten: "Be aware of wonder." Actually, children don't have to learn that one. They come programmed with it. With all five senses unatrophied and full of natural curiosity, a child can't help wondering about everything around him. I have sometimes wished that each of my three grandsons would stop asking questions for just five minutes. But the fault is mine, not theirs. Wondering why the roots go down and the plants go up is fundamental. Thank goodness they do. We all need roots for balance and something to reach up for.

It's never too late.

It Still Happens in Vermont

In spite of the gloom and doom we read and hear about every day, I am heartened by the little kindnesses that still happen but that rarely get media coverage.

Cary Tordiff, who plows out our driveway, had slim pickings one winter because we had very few heavy snows. Instead we had several periods of thawing and freezing, which turned our driveway into a hockey rink. One morning I heard his truck and looked out to see him shoveling sand onto our icy driveway from the back of his truck. There was no plowable snow, but he figured we might have trouble staying upright, so he sanded it, giving us welcome traction for boots and tires.

For many years two very elderly ladies lived in a little house down the road. Margaret Snyder was in her midnineties and her friend Nellie McClure, reached 101 before she died last year. In their last years here, they had Meals on Wheels delivered to them each weekday and a relative came to visit each Sunday. But a neighbor, Clara Manor, whose own house bulged with children and grandchildren on Christmas and Thanksgiving, always fixed up holiday meals with all the trimmings, and whatever Manor daughters were home would take them over to the little white house for Nellie and Margaret.

One item that did hit the papers delighted me. A couple in Burlington were driving along Williston Road when they saw several bags fall out of an armored truck ahead of them. They stopped, picked up the bags, and drove directly to the police station, where the bags turned out to contain many thousands of dollars. What pleased me was that the couple said it never occurred to them to do anything else. They knew it had to be money. They knew it wasn't theirs, and that was that. I'm glad they live in my world.

An unfortunate robbery happened in Colchester. A Girl Scout troop leader was sitting in her car at the post office counting the money the Girl Scouts had earned selling cookies so that she could get a money order. Suddenly a man reached in through her open window, grabbed the $2,000, and fled. Two days later, a Burlington couple donated $400 to the Girl Scout Council because they had read that $364 of the $2,000 was to go to the troop for the girls' merit badges. The girls not only got their merit badges, they also had a roller-skating party.

These things could have happened anywhere, but I'm glad they happened in Vermont. I continue to believe that the average person cares for his fellow man. When robberies stop being news, then I'll worry.

Project Home is another example of people reaching out

to each other. They match up an older or handicapped person who wants to remain in his own home with a younger or able-bodied person who needs a place to live in exchange for help around the house, shopping, or whatever has become difficult for the homeowner. Right up our road an elderly widower who was not well was able to stay in his own home and eventually to die there because Anna, a Czechoslovakian woman with limited English, moved in, tended the garden, cooked, cleaned, and made her home there for two years. They were an unlikely couple who would never have met except for Project Home.

The return of spring always reaffirms my faith in human nature. Performing the old rites of spring again is comforting, as is planting the first seeds of spinach, lettuce and radishes, even though the soil is still cool and in Coleridge's words, "the spring comes slowly up this way." So is tapping a few maple trees because you know that once again the sap is rising and soon every maple twig will be laced out with tiny red flowers. Cleaning out our old spring, pulling away the dead leaves, resetting the stones and watching the water clear is a rite honored in Robert Frost's "The Pasture." This spring, halfway down the path, has never stopped running in the forty years we have lived here. The old house next to our present one was built in 1820, and the spring fed the big square watering trough where the Nealy's cows drank. It always flows at the same rate (unless it gets clogged up in the early spring), as it has for 170 years, through flood or drought.

It is reassuring to celebrate spring in other familiar ways. We still color Easter eggs, but now they are for Morgan to hunt with the same eagerness that Patty and Debbie exhibited a generation before. I always have to check out the wood anemones in the same spot across the road, and there is a hidden hollow up the road where a small patch of trailing arbutus is holding its own against the barrage of gravel and salt and snow that almost covers it each winter. The song sparrows have returned to glean the sunflower seeds dropped by the chickadees, and a newly awakened little chipmunk scampers across the big boulder.

Quotations from the older poets pop uninvited into my mind, like Browning's ebullient

> The year's at the spring
> And day's at the morn;
> Morning's at seven:
> The hillside's dew-pearled;
> The lark's on the wing
> The snail's on the thorn:
> God's in his heaven—
> All's right with the world.

All may not be right with the world, but as Shelley, even in a troubled mood, wrote, "If winter comes, can spring be far behind?"

In spring a sign is enough, another chance, a fresh start, and the burgeoning of hope for peace in this beautiful and fragile world.

About the Author

Born in Montclair, New Jersey, Maggie Wolf is a Vermonter by choice rather than by birth. But she does have one foot wedged firmly in the door by virtue of two Vermont great-grandfathers. After graduation from Mount Holyoke College and the Bank Street College of Education, she taught at the Bank Street Nursery School and Sarah Lawrence College. And in 1939 Maggie married a young dedicated doctor George A. Wolf, Jr.

Maggie's first book appeared twenty-five years ago, and she hasn't stopped writing since. She is the author of five other New England Press books and regularly writes articles in which she shares her love of Vermont and her secrets of the joys of country living.

The Wolfs bought their farm in Jericho in 1948, summering there until 1952 when George was appointed dean of the University of Vermont College of Medicine and they became "year round summer folk." Nine years later they moved to Boston for five years and then on to Kansas City for four years, but they always returned with their daughters to Jericho in the summer—even if only for one month.

In 1970 they saw the handwriting on the walls of Jericho and returned to Vermont for keeps. The family census has changed since 1948. Patty is now Mrs. Tage Strōm and lives in New Fairfield, Connecticut, with her Finnish husband and two sons, Patrick and Peter. Debbie is now Mrs. Stephen Page and lives in Williston, Vermont, with her husband and son, Morgan. In June 1990, George, Maggie's loving partner and companion for more than fifty years, passed away. Today Maggie lives in the house she and George built right alongside the original old farmhouse they fell in love with back in 1948.

About the Illustrator

A native of Colorado, Mary MacDonnell studied art at Maryland Art Institute and Parsons School of Design. She worked for some time as a children's fashion illustrator in New York City where she met and married John MacDonnell, an Englishman. Following the lure of country living, they moved to Blandford, Massachusetts, and a 200-year-old farmhouse where they raised four children and an assortment of horses, dogs, and cats.

Well known in the Berkshire hilltowns for her many artistic talents, Mary is best known for her pen and ink portraits of old New England homes. She began working in watercolors two years ago and now exhibits both her pen and inks and watercolors in area juried shows.